FATIMA
and
OUR
SALVATION

ISBN   0 85172 737 9

Imprimi potest: Manuel Vaz Pato, S.J., Provincial

Imprimatur: ✠ Eurica Dias Nogueira, Archbishop and Primate,
                    Braga, Portugal

Printed and bound

by

Billings & Sons Ltd,
Worcester

and published April 1985

by

AUGUSTINE PUBLISHING COMPANY

CHULMLEIGH, DEVON, EX18 7HL

FATIMA

and

OUR SALVATION

by

Father Antonio Maria Martins, S.J.

Translated by the Dominican Nuns of the
Perpetual Rosary, Fatima

Christmas 1985 from
Sr. Rosario

AUGUSTINE
DILIGITE HOMINES
INTERFICITE ERRORES
Publishing Company

DEVON, MCMLXXXV

"Pray, pray, a great deal, and make sacrifices for sinners, for many souls go to Hell because they have no one to make sacrifices and pray for them."

—Our Lady of Fatima

CONTENTS

v

Contents

Author's Preface

Much has been written about what could be the theme or the soul of the Message of Fatima.

For some, it is the devotion to the Immaculate Heart of Mary; for others, it is war and peace in the world; for the majority, it is penance and prayer.

The three opinions are valid and there are solid arguments to sustain them.

As for me, it seems that all these subjects can be incorporated directly or indirectly into the mystery of the Mystical Body of Christ and our role in the salvation of souls.

I deem it unnecessary to devote a chapter to expounding the theology of the Mystical Body. It is a doctrinal point developed by St. Paul through his letters, following on the revelation made to him, that to persecute Christians is to persecute Christ Himself.

There is a mysterious reality revealed to us by the Son of God: "On that day you will understand that I am in the Father and you in me and I in you" (*Jn.* 14:20); "He who eats my flesh and drinks my blood lives in me and I in him." (*Jn.* 6:57).

Sister Lucia, in her Fourth Memoir, describing the first apparition, without any pretensions to a display of theology, says with all naturalness, "As she spoke these last words (i.e., 'the grace of God will be your comfort'), she opened her hands for the first time, and from the palms came two streams of light so intense that they penetrated our breasts and reached the most intimate parts of our souls, making us

vii

see ourselves in God, who is that light, more clearly than in the best of mirrors." (A. M. Martins, *Documentos de Fatima,* Porto 1976, p. 332).

This union with Christ is so profound and so intimate that it led St. Paul to write to the Christians of Rome: "When we were baptised we went into the tomb with him and joined him in death, so that as Christ was raised from the dead by the Father's glory, we too might live a new life. If in union with Christ we have imitated his death, we shall also imitate him in his resurrection" (*Rom.* 6:4-5); and to those of Corinth: "Just as a human body, though it is made up of many parts, is a single unit because all these parts, though many, make one body, so is it with Christ." (*1 Cor.* 12:12). Therefore, we ought to "rejoice with those who rejoice and be sad with those in sorrow." (*Rom.* 12:15).

If Jesus Christ is Head of this mysterious Body which, for this same reason, is called the *Mystical* Body, and if all of us are members of this Body, then each one has his own proper function to fulfill here on earth, according to the gifts received. In Heaven, we will continue to be united in the praise of the Blessed Trinity and in intercession on behalf of those who are still struggling in this "valley of tears."

This is the function of the Blessed Virgin Mary: "By her maternal charity, she cares for the brethren of her Son, who still journey on earth surrounded by dangers and difficulties, until they are led into their blessed home. Therefore, the Blessed Virgin is invoked in the Church under the titles of Advocate, Helper, Benefactress, and Mediatrix." (*Lumen Gentium,* 62).

Owing to her dignity as Mother of Jesus, Head of the Mystical Body, her intercession has, one might almost say, omnipotent force.

We shall see further on, principally in the two succeeding studies in this series, *Fatima—Way of Peace* and *Fatima and the Heart of Mary,* that in order to escape war, it is necessary, besides other requirements, to pray the Rosary.

The Eternal Father, in His ways which are not like ours, so disposes things that we do not fall into the temptation of putting aside or marginalizing she who is, after Christ, the masterpiece of His hands.

No member of the Mystical Body can be despised with impunity. Jesus considers as done to Himself what we do to others, and we sin by omission against His Person when we willfully fail to come to the aid of those in need.

With how much greater reason, then, He counts as done to Himself what we do to His most Holy Mother. Is she not the most excellent, the most privileged member of the Mystical Body? And because He wants to see her honoured as He honoured her, He makes the peace of the world depend on the observance of His commandments and the homage paid, as we shall see, to the Immaculate Heart of Mary.

I think, therefore, that it is not inopportune to envision the Message of Fatima as being intimately penetrated and shaped by the Mystery of the Mystical Body. In fact, it is owing to this divine reality that our prayer and penance are required and are of value.

As members of the same Body, we are bound to each other in solidarity. We are beneficiaries of the merits of Christ and of the Saints' acts of virtue. On the other hand, sinful acts which deserve punishment affect, to a certain degree, all the members. If in Sodom and Gomorrha there had been ten just men, those cities would not have been destroyed. David sinned and "seventy thousand men of the people died." (*2 Sam.* 24:15).

In the Message of Fatima we are told that the miracle was less imposing because of the Administrator's sin. (*Documentos de Fatima,* p. 501).

In the present work, which is destined for the general public and not just for those at university level, I shall deal first of all with "The Power of Prayer," and in the second and more extensive part with "The Message of Fatima."

In the first section, that on prayer, my object is to demonstrate, from Our Lord's own words about it in the Gospels, the power of prayer to move God to attend to our requests, and how we must pray with the right attitudes and objectives so that our prayers will bear fruit.

Prayer is at the very heart of the Message of Fatima. Right from the first apparition of the Angel, the children were invited to pray, and Our Lady underlined its importance in the sight of God when, six times in succession, she told them to pray the Rosary.

Hence, when we understand prayer correctly we will be able to apply it in our personal lives in the way that God desires of every member of the Mystical Body of Christ, according to the Message of Fatima, and this is the theme which forms the second part of my study.

As it is not a matter of a scholarly thesis, but rather a simple exposition of a subject that I consider of great value for the spiritual life, it is natural that there may be some considerations and even digressions which would not be permitted in an academic work.

Nevertheless, I shall seek to be exact in the quotations from the sources of the texts chosen, so that anyone may be able to verify the authenticity of my interpretations.

I

THE POWER OF PRAYER

In the Gospels, there is no point on which Jesus Christ insisted so much as on the power of prayer.

It is significant that at the Last Supper—when the Son of God spoke out of the abundance of His heart, like the dying father giving his last recommendations— he guaranteed, no less than four times, that our prayers would be heard.

These are His words referring to the power of our prayer, inserted in their proper context:

"The words I say to you I do not speak as from myself: it is the Father, living in me who is doing this work. You must believe me when I say that I am in the Father and the Father is in me; believe it on the evidence of this work, if for no other reason. I tell you most solemnly, whoever believes in me will perform the same works as I do myself, he will perform even greater works, because I am going to the Father." (*Jn.* 14:10-12). *"Whatever you ask for in my name I will do, so that the Father may be glorified in the Son. If you ask for anything in my name, I will do it."* (*Jn.* 14:10-14).

"I am the vine, you are the branches. Whoever remains in me, with me in him, bears fruit in plenty; for cut off from me you can do nothing. Anyone who does not remain in me is like a branch that has been thrown away—he withers; these branches are collected and thrown on the fire, and they are burnt. *If you remain in me and my words remain in you, you may ask what you will and you shall get it."* (*Jn.* 15:5-7).

1

"You are my friends, if you do what I command you. I shall not call you servants any more, because a servant does not know his master's business; I call you friends, because I have made known to you everything I have learnt from my Father. You did not choose me, no, I chose you; and I commissioned you to go out and to bear fruit, fruit that will last; *and then the Father will give you anything you ask him in my name.*" (*Jn.* 15:14-16).

"A woman in childbirth suffers, because her time has come; but when she has given birth to the child she forgets the suffering in her joy that a man has been born into the world. So it is with you: you are sad now, but I shall see you again, and your hearts will be full of joy, and that joy no one shall take from you. When that day comes, you will not ask me any questions. *I tell you most solemnly, anything you ask for from the Father he will grant in my name. Until now you have not asked for anything in my name. Ask and you will receive, and so your joy will be complete.*" (*Jn.* 16:21-24).

This last phrase spoken by Our Lord does not seem to have anything to do with what He had said beforehand, but came out as something that overflowed from His heart. Indeed, the four passages cited above reveal that the Lord ardently desired to impress on the souls of the Apostles confidence in the power of prayer. This was an idea that had for a long time been part of His teaching. In fact, St. Luke relates that one of the disciples asked the Master to teach them to pray. Jesus responded with the words of the *Our Father,* and immediately after, He told them this parable:

"Suppose one of you has a friend and goes to him in the middle of the night to say, 'My friend, lend me three loaves, because a friend of mine on his travels has just arrived at my house and I have nothing to offer him'; and the man answers from inside the house, 'Do not bother me. The door is bolted now, and my children and I are in bed; I cannot get up to give it to you.' I tell you, if the man does not get up and give it to him for friendship's sake, persistence will be enough to make him get up and give his friend all he wants. So I say to you: *Ask, and it will be given to you; search, and you will find; knock, and the door will be opened to you. For the one who asks always receives; the one who searches always finds; the one who knocks will always have the door opened to him.* What father among you would hand his son a stone when he asked for bread? Or hand him a snake instead of a fish? Or hand him a scorpion if he asked for an egg? If you then, who are evil, know how to give your children what is good, *how much more will the heavenly Father give the Holy Spirit to those who ask him!"* (*Lk.* 11:5-13).

This was not the only parable about prayer recorded by St. Luke. He recounts two more for us in the 18th chapter of his Gospel:

"Then he told them a parable about the need to pray continually and never lose heart. 'There was a judge in a certain town,' he said, 'who had neither fear of God nor respect for man. In the same town there was a widow who kept on coming to him and saying, "I want justice from you against my enemy!" For a long time he refused, but at last he said to himself, "Maybe I have neither fear of God nor respect for man, but since she keeps pestering me I must give this widow her just rights, or she will persist in coming and worry me to death."' And the Lord said, 'You notice what the unjust judge has to say? Now will not God see justice done to his chosen who cry to him day and night even when he delays to help them? I promise you, he will see justice done to them, and done speedily. But when the Son of Man comes, will he find any faith on earth?'

"He spoke the following parable to some people who prided themselves on being virtuous and despised everyone else. 'Two men went up to the Temple to pray, one a Pharisee, the other a tax collector. The Pharisee stood there and said this prayer to himself, "I thank you, God, that I am not grasping, unjust, adulterous like the rest of mankind, and particularly that I am not like this tax collector here. I fast twice a week; I pay tithes on all I get." The tax collec-

tor stood some distance away, not daring even to raise his
eyes to heaven; but he beat his breast and said, "God, be
merciful to me, a sinner." This man, I tell you, went home
again at rights with God; the other did not. For everyone
who exalts himself will be humbled, but the man who hum-
bles himself will be exalted.'"

The Example of Christ

According to His usual manner of procedure, Jesus did
not limit Himself to recommending that we ought to pray,
but He left us His own example. In fact, it can be affirmed
without hesitation that Christ was the prototype of the praying man. He prayed much during His earthly life and continues in Heaven to intercede for us with the Father:

"I am writing this, my children, to stop you sinning; but
if anyone should sin, we have our Advocate with the
Father, Jesus Christ, who is just." (*1 Jn.* 2:1). St. Paul cor-
roborates this exactly: "Jesus Christ . . . there at God's right
hand stands and pleads for us." (*Rom.* 8:34).

And what does the Lord do, hidden in all the tabernacles
of the earth, but intercede for us unceasingly?

Now if we retrace our steps in time across almost two
thousand years, and scrutinize with the eyes of our imagination the dwellings of the Holy Family in Egypt and in
Nazareth, we will see that Jesus, from childhood, praised
God in the arms of Mary Immaculate or on the bosom of
the just man Joseph: "Your will is my heritage for ever, the
joy of my heart. I set myself to carry out your statutes in
fullness, for ever." (*Ps.* 118:111-112).

Who could discover what would have been the intimate
prayer of Jesus, Mary and Joseph?

Surely the reading of Sacred Scripture would have been
Jesus' greatest joy as "He increased in wisdom, in stature,
and in favour with God and men." (*Lk.* 2:52).

The books of the Old Testament were undoubtedly the primer where, from His Mother's arms, the Child Jesus learned to spell.

How His heart was stirred on hearing Mary and Joseph read the sacred books, which were to attain complete fulfillment in His divine Person! (cf. *Lk.* 4:18-21).

When He began His public life by undergoing John's baptism, St. Luke tells us that "Jesus was at prayer." (*Lk.* 3:21). Afterwards, the Holy Spirit led Him into the wilderness where He gave Himself to prayer and fasting for forty days and forty nights.

The Gospels furnish us with very significant data about Jesus' habitual procedure in what regarded His apostolic activity and reservation of time for prayer: "His reputation continued to grow, and large crowds would gather to hear him and to have their sickness cured, but he would always go off to some place where he could be alone and pray." (*Lk.* 5:15-16). "Now it was about this time that he went out into the hills to pray; and he spent the whole night in prayer to God." (*Lk.* 6:12).

Other texts could be quoted, but these are sufficient to convince us that, if we wish to be Christ's disciples, we must needs devote some minutes, at least, to prayer each day.

Qualities of Prayer

Jesus Christ, through His living example and His teaching by means of parables, has left us indications as to the qualities which should mould our prayer in order to be heard: humility, perseverance, faith.

Before God, of ourselves, we are nothing. From Him we have received everything, from our creation to our preservation in existence and the gifts we possess. How is it then that we dare to make demands on the Lord of the Universe?

Now one of the more subtle requirements that our sub-conscious leads us to impose on God is that He should grant us what we ask immediately, or in a short space of time. Frequently, because this does not happen, innumerable people leave off praying and, what is worse, nurture an attitude of interior revolt against God.

The parable of the unjust judge relates that he refused *for a long time* to attend to the poor widow, but she persisted and finally obtained what she wanted.

The humble person asks without imposing conditions of any kind, being fully conformed to the will of God, who knows what is good for us. We are not aware of it, but it often happens that we resemble a child who cries because it is denied a knife or some other object that may cause it harm.

Jesus Christ is a sublime model of what our attitude ought to be before God: "He then left to make his way as usual to the Mount of Olives ... and knelt down and prayed. 'Father,' he said, 'if you are willing, take this cup away from me. Nevertheless, let your will be done, not mine.'" (*Lk*. 22:39-42). And this full conformity with His Father's will obtained for Him what He asked, as the author of the Letter to the Hebrews asserts: "Christ, during his life on earth, offered up prayer and entreaty, aloud and in silent tears, to the one who had the power to save him out of death, and he submitted so humbly that his prayer was heard." (*Heb*. 5:7).

How can this phrase of the inspired text be explained?

All biblical commentators agree that the response lies in the glorious Resurrection of the Son of Man.

In the most sorrowful hours of Gethsemane, He made humble supplication to the Father to remove the chalice of the Passion, and the Father heard Him, by giving Him strength to carry the cross to Calvary, and freeing Him from the bonds of death through His triumphant Resurrection on Easter Sunday morning.

God always listens to our supplications. If He does not

grant exactly what we ask, He bestows on us something better. He acts like a mother who refuses a dangerous object to her little one and gives it a kiss instead, or a harmless toy.

It is not without reason that Scripture alerts us to the fact that "we cannot choose words in order to pray properly." (*Rom.* 8:26). We allow ourselves to be carried away by the apparent urgency of our needs and situations. A mother, troubled because of a child who is seriously ill, only thinks of restoring it to health. She does not see anything that could be better for it. God, however, who is our Father, who has before His eyes the past, the present and the future of all His creatures, knows what is best for it. Let us suppose that this afflicted mother could see that in the future her beloved child would be guilty of the most dreadful crimes. In such a case, would she make all the promises she does in order to obtain her child's health?

For this reason, whenever we request temporal favours, we should always include the condition: "Lord, I ask this of You, if it be for Your glory and the spiritual good of my soul."

Faith and Confidence

To obtain what we ask we must have faith in the Person to whom we are praying. We are not addressing an abstract being, but we are speaking with a *Person* who loves us. It is necessary to have faith in this Person, in His power, in His love. Jesus replied to the centurion who desired the cure of a servant: "Go back, then; you have believed, so let this be done for you." (*Mt.* 8:13). And to the two blind men who shouted, "Take pity on us, Son of David," He put the question, "Do you believe I can do this?" They replied, "Sir, we do." Then He touched their eyes, saying, "Your faith deserves it, so let this be done for you." (*Mt.* 9:27-29).

And to the Canaanite woman, whom He had treated with

unaccustomed harshness, He spoke these words of praise and recompense: "Woman, you have great faith. Let your wish be granted." (*Mt.* 15:26-28).

On the contrary, He was surprised, and He denounced the lack of faith shown by the people and His disciples: "He was amazed at their lack of faith." (*Mk.* 6:6). "So they went to him and woke him, saying, 'Save us, Lord, we are going down!' And he said to them, 'Why are you so frightened, you men of little faith?'" (*Mt.* 8:25-26).

He did not perform miracles where there was lack of faith: "And he did not work many miracles there because of their lack of faith." (*Mt.* 13:58).

He promised that a petition made with faith would be efficacious: "I tell you solemnly, if your faith were the size of a mustard seed you could say to this mountain, 'Move from here to there,' and it would move; nothing would be impossible for you." (*Mt.* 17:19).

On another occasion He worked a miracle and insisted on the same idea: "As he was returning to the city in the early morning, he felt hungry. Seeing a fig tree by the road, he went up to it and found nothing on it but leaves. And he said to it, 'May you never bear fruit again'; and at that instant the fig tree withered. The disciples were amazed when they saw it. 'What happened to the tree,' they said, 'that it withered there and then?' Jesus answered, 'I tell you solemnly, if you have faith and do not doubt at all, not only will you do what I have done to the fig tree, but even if you say to this mountain, "Get up and throw yourself into the sea," it will be done. And if you have faith, everything you ask for in prayer you will receive.'" (*Mt.* 21:18-22).

It is necessary, therefore, to pray, but with faith and trust in God, who is the Father Almighty and who loves us as children.

What We Should Pray For

Jesus Christ not only insisted that we ought to pray, but even suggested some intentions for which we ought to pray. Hence St. Matthew relates that the Master "made a tour through all the towns and villages, teaching in their synagogues, proclaiming the Good News of the kingdom and curing all kinds of diseases and sickness. And when he saw the crowds he felt sorry for them because they were harassed and dejected, like sheep without a shepherd. Then he said to his disciples, 'The harvest is rich but the labourers are few, so ask the Lord of the harvest to send labourers into his harvest.'" (*Mt.* 9:35-38).

In these verses, the mystery of our participation in the salvific work of Christ is set forth. In fact, at the Last Supper, He declared to His Apostles, "It is not you who have chosen me, but I have chosen you." A vocation is a divine gift, but the Lord of the harvest wishes to be asked before sending fresh labourers to the harvesting.

Christ is the Head of the Mystical Body, but He acts through the members. Actually, God's way of acting in the universe is to make use of secondary causes, in such a manner that His presence or activity passes unperceived by the majority of men. They think, therefore, that they are masters of their own destiny, and there is no need of God at all.

Poor blind ones! St. Paul was right when he wrote almost two thousand years ago, "Ever since God created the world, his everlasting power and deity—however invisible—have been there for the mind to see in the things he has made. That is why such people are without excuse: they knew God and yet refused to honour him as God or to thank him; instead, they made nonsense out of logic and their empty minds were darkened. The more they called themselves philosophers, the more stupid they grew ... That is why God has abandoned them to degrading passions: why their women have turned from natural intercourse to unnatural practices and why their menfolk have given up natural intercourse to be consumed with passion for each other, men doing shameless things with men and getting an appropriate reward for their perversion ... Libellers, slanderers, enemies of God, rude, arrogant and boastful, enterprising in sin, rebellious to parents, without brains, honour, love or pity. They know what God's verdict is: that those who behave like this deserve to die—and yet they do it; and what is worse, encourage others to do the same." (*Rom.* 1:20-32).

It would seem that the Apostle is describing the world situation of our times! This should impel us to pray fervently every day, as the Lord has exhorted us, so that His hand may be upon us and not permit us to be led astray by such repulsive vices. And if we have the misfortune to fall from time to time into some grave sin, let us beg Him, with great humility and confidence, to help us rise again without delay and amend our life.

He who promised so many times that our prayers would be heard, will certainly grant our request if we ask the grace to be liberated from the state of grave sin, to abandon some vice which is enslaving us or some fault that is dragging us down and preventing us from attaining the holiness that God expects of us.

Vocation to Holiness

From the very first books of the Old Testament up to the last of the New, the sacred pages exhort us to be holy. Here are some passages: "For I am the Lord your God! Be holy because I am holy." (*Lev.* 11:44). "The Lord spoke to Moses, saying, 'Speak to the whole community of the sons of Israel and say to them: Be holy, for I, the Lord your God, am holy.'" (*Lev.* 19:1-2).

St. Peter, in writing to the Christians of Asia Minor, reminds them, "Be holy in all you do, since it is the Holy One who has called you, and scripture says: Be holy, for I am holy." (*1 Pt.* 1:15-16).

St. Paul, in his turn, when addressing the different churches, insists on the same idea, and thus commences his Letter to the Christians of Ephesus and surrounding communities in these words: "From Paul, appointed by God to be an apostle of Christ Jesus, to the saints at Ephesus who are faithful to Christ Jesus: Grace and peace to you from God our Father and from the Lord Jesus Christ. Blessed be God the Father of our Lord Jesus Christ, who has blessed us with all the spiritual blessings of heaven in Christ. Before the world was made, he chose us, chose us in Christ, to be holy and spotless, and to live through love in his presence." (*Eph.* 1:1-4).

And in his first Letter to the Christians of Thessalonica, now called Salonica, his words are incisive: "For this is the will of God, your sanctification." (*1 Th.* 4:3).

To the community of Colossae, a town between Ephesus and Laodicaea, he writes, "You are God's chosen race, his saints; he loves you, and you should be clothed in sincere compassion, in kindness and humility, gentleness and patience. Bear with one another; forgive each other as soon as a quarrel begins. The Lord has forgiven you; now you must do the same. Over all these clothes, to keep them together and complete them, put on love. And may the peace of Christ reign in your hearts, because it is for this that you were called together as parts of one body." (*Col.* 3:12-15).

Jesus sums up all these biblical teachings in one phrase: "You must therefore be perfect just as your heavenly Father is perfect." (*Mt.* 5:48).

To God, the one thing that matters in this world is holiness. That is why, in choosing a woman to be the Mother of His Son, He did not exalt her with riches or other temporal possessions which we so ambitiously desire, but He endowed her with the privilege of the Immaculate Conception; that is, He exempted her from all sin, including original sin.

In the eyes of God what counts is holiness, for it is

through holiness that we resemble Him.

Well then, if God wants us to be holy, and on the other hand assures us that He will grant what we ask of Him, why do we doubt? Why do we not beg Him every day: Lord, grant me the grace of being better today than yesterday, of corresponding more fully to Your designs of love in my regard?

Let us remember that great sinners became the great Saints whom we venerate at our altars. Divine grace is omnipotent. Jesus assures us that "things that are impossible for men are possible for God." (*Lk.* 18:27). If it seems impossible for us to forgive one who has seriously offended us, let us ask the Lord for this grace, and sentiments of pardon will inundate our spirit.

There are many divorces in the world, much hostility, rancour, revenge, because people do not pray. If spouses, at the first flare of serious misunderstanding, knelt to ask the Heavenly Father for light and help, the tempest would blow over at once, and there would be fewer children psychologically ruined through parental conflicts.

But let us not, in our prayers, think only of ourselves. Christ has admonished us to pray for others: "Ask the Lord of the harvest to send labourers to his harvest." (*Mt.* 9:38).

Priestly Vocations

Here is an intention which, in spite of the fact that it was explicitly recommended by Our Lord, is mostly forgotten nowadays. How many families pray daily for priestly vocations? Many seminaries are empty because there is no prayer for this intention. There are many parishes without a priest, and within a brief period of time many others will be at a loss, for want of a substitute to replace those who depart this life.

But this lack of clergy leads us to the consideration of

another more serious problem. I refer to the salvation of souls who live in pagan lands, and who make up the greater part of the world's population.

The Church becomes day by day more unable to evangelize the world, for its population is increasing by such proportions that it is humanly impossible to provide sufficient missionaries for all the inhabitants of the earth.

Is the greater part of humanity then condemned?

By no means, because God wills the salvation of all. And He Himself guarantees this: "As I live, says the Lord God, I take pleasure, not in the death of a wicked man, but in the turning back of a wicked man who changes his ways to win life." (*Ez.* 33:11). "To do this is right, and will please God our Saviour: He wants everyone to be saved and reach full knowledge of the truth." (*1 Tim.* 2:3-4).

The solution to this mysterious problem lies in the power of prayer: *"Whatever you ask for in my name I will do, so that the Father may be glorified in the Son. If you ask for anything in my name, I will do it."* (*Jn.* 14:13-14).

The salvation of our brothers is in our hands!

This responsibility which rests on our shoulders is placed in high relief, most impressively, in the Message of Fatima, not only through the words of the Angel and of the Blessed Virgin, but, as we shall see, through the life lived by the three little shepherds.

The Holy Father

Another intention most pleasing to God is undoubtedly that we pray to Him for the Holy Father. Indeed, the Acts of the Apostles provide us with a very explicit account of the power of the prayer of Christians, when Herod began to persecute the pillars of the Church: "It was about this time that King Herod started persecuting certain members of the Church. He beheaded James the brother of John, and when he saw that this pleased the Jews he decided to arrest Peter as well . . . He put Peter in prison, assigning four squads of four soldiers each to guard him in turns. Herod meant to try Peter in public after the end of Passover week. All the time Peter was under guard the Church prayed to God for him unremittingly. On the night before Herod was to try him, Peter was sleeping between two soldiers, fastened with double chains, while guards kept watch at the main entrance to the prison. Then suddenly the angel of the Lord stood there, and the cell was filled with light. He tapped Peter on the side and woke him. 'Get up!' he said. 'Hurry!'—and the chains fell from his hands. The angel then said . . . 'Wrap your cloak round you and follow me.' . . . They passed through two guard posts one after the other, and reached the iron gate leading to the city. This opened of its own accord." (*Acts* 12:1-10).

The Church prayed and God worked a miracle! Something similar has happened in our days with the diabolical attack on the Holy Father, Peter's successor! The gates of Hell did not prevail nor will they prevail, because God is omnipotent! But He wants our participation in the triumph of Good over evil, by means of humble and persevering prayer.

The practice of praying and offering sacrifices for the Holy Father is one of the characteristics of Jacinta's piety. Let us hear what Lucia relates:

"Two priests who came to question us recommended that we pray for the Holy Father. Jacinta asked who the Holy Father was, and the good priests explained to us who he was and how much he needed our prayers. Jacinta had such an intense love for the Holy Father then, that whenever she offered her sacrifices to Jesus she added, 'and for the Holy Father.' At the end of her Rosary she always said three Hail Marys for the Holy Father, and sometimes she would remark, 'I wish I could see the Holy Father! So many people come here but the Holy Father never does!'

"When, some time later, we were put in prison, what

made Jacinta suffer most was to feel that their parents had abandoned them. With tears streaming down her cheeks, she would say:

'Neither your parents nor mine have come to see us. They don't bother about us any more!'

'Don't cry,' said Francisco, 'we can offer this to Jesus for sinners.'

"Then, raising his eyes and hands to Heaven, he made the offering, 'O my Jesus, this is for love of You, and for the conversion of sinners.' Jacinta added, 'And also for the Holy Father, and in reparation for the sins committed against the Immaculate Heart of Mary.'

"After being separated for awhile, we were re-united in one of the other rooms of the prison. When they told us they were coming soon to take us away to be fried alive, Jacinta went aside and stood by a window overlooking the cattle market. I thought at first she was trying to distract her thoughts with the view, but I soon realized that she was crying. I went over and drew her close to me, asking her why she was crying:

'Because we are going to die,' she replied, 'without ever seeing our parents again, not even our mothers!' With tears running down her cheeks, she added, 'I would like at least to see my mother.'

'Don't you want, then, to offer this sacrifice for the conversion of sinners?'

'I do want to, I do!' With her face bathed in tears, she joined her hands, raised her eyes to Heaven and made her offering: 'O my Jesus! This is for love of You, for the conversion of sinners, for the Holy Father, and in reparation for the sins committed against the Immaculate Heart of Mary!'" (*Documentos de Fatima*, pp. 48-52).

Let us make our own this prayer of the lovable Jacinta.

Unity of the Churches and Peace

Far be it from me to attempt to put forward a complete list of intentions which we ought to remember in our daily prayers. But I cannot omit to mention two more which seem to me to be very important and pleasing to God. I refer to the unity of all Christians and to peace.

We know that, at the Last Supper, Jesus prayed to His Father for these intentions: "Holy Father, keep those you have given me true to your name, so that they may be one like us... I pray not only for these, but for those also who through their words will believe in me. May they all be one. Father, may they be one in us, as you are in me and I am in you, so that the world may believe it was you who sent me. I have given them the glory you gave to me, that they may be one as we are one. With me in them and you in me, may they be so completely one that the world will realise that it was you who sent me and that I have loved them as much as you loved me." (*Jn.* 17:11, 20-23).

If Jesus, Head of the Mystical Body, prayed so intensely to the Father that we all might be one, how is it that we, members of that same Body, do not pray for this unity? Further, is not this one of the great objectives of the Church, above all in these latter years, with the efforts being made in the ecumenical field? Furthermore, it is universally held that His Holiness, Pope John Paul II, is the providential person to accomplish this union, and he undoubtedly prays for this intention every day. Let us be united with the Holy Father in praying daily for the unity of all Christians.

If, on the other hand, all Christians or all the baptized made a serious effort to live in accordance with the teachings of Christ, it would be easier to obtain peace for the world. At any rate, this is the additional intention which should preoccupy everyone, especially the young. When we attend Holy Mass, therefore, let us accompany the celebrant with redoubled fervour in the prayers in which he implores:

"May all of us who share in the Body and Blood of Christ be brought together in unity by the Holy Spirit."

"Deliver us, Lord, from every evil, and grant us peace in our day."

"Lamb of God, You take away the sins of the world: Grant us peace."

The theme of peace will be more amply developed in the next title in this series: *Fatima—Way of Peace.*

II

THE MESSAGE OF FATIMA

The Message of Fatima pertains to the apparitions of the Angel and of Our Lady in the Cova da Iria, in Pontevedra and in Tuy, as well as to the example of the heroic lives of Jacinta and Francisco, whose Causes of Beatification are progressing in Rome.

To clear up, right away, the ambiguities of those who persist in not accepting any other than the apparitions of Our Lady in 1917, attributing those of Pontevedra and of Tuy to Sister Lucia's imagination, it is opportune to point out the following:

1. *The authority of the Church has never placed these apparitions in doubt;* rather the contrary, it has given implicit signs of accepting them. Consequently, Pius XII consecrated the world to the Immaculate Heart of Mary on 31 October 1942, using a formula in which there was a very clear allusion to Russia: "To peoples separated by error and discord, namely, those who profess singular devotion to you, where there was no house that did not display your holy icon, today hidden perhaps until better days, give them peace, and lead them again to the only flock of Christ under the true and only Shepherd." On 7 July 1952, he explicitly consecrated "all the peoples of Russia to the same Immaculate Heart." (A.A.S.44-1952-511).

John Paul II, in his homily of 13 May 1982, made mention of the acts of his predecessor in these very significant words: "The appeal of the Lady of the Message of Fatima is so deeply rooted in the Gospel and the whole of Tradition

18

that the Church feels that the message imposes a commitment on her. She has responded through the Servant of God Pius XII (whose episcopal ordination took place precisely on 13 May 1917): He consecrated the human race and especially the peoples of Russia to the Immaculate Heart of Mary. Was not that consecration his response to the evangelical eloquence of the call of Fatima?"

Now Our Lady's request, that the Holy Father in union with all the Bishops should consecrate the world and Russia to her Immaculate Heart, reached Pius XII through the famous letter from Sister Lucia written in Tuy on 2 December 1940. In this document, Lucia refers to the apparitions of Pontevedra and Tuy. She says expressly, "In 1929, through another apparition, Our Lady asked for the consecration of Russia to her Immaculate Heart, promising its conversion through this means and the hindering of the propagation of its errors." (*Documentos de Fatima,* p. 436).

If three Popes—Pius XII, Paul VI* and John Paul II— made and renewed the consecration of the world and Russia to the Immaculate Heart of Mary, and gave such importance to it; if the present Pope says explicitly that "the Church, feeling that the message imposed a commitment on her, responded through the Servant of God Pius XII, who consecrated the human race and especially the peoples of Russia to the Immaculate Heart of Mary"; and if the request to make this consecration of Russia reached the Vatican through the above-mentioned letter from Sister Lucia, then it is more than obvious that the Supreme Pontiffs have had no doubts regarding the apparitions at Pontevedra and Tuy to the humble religious.

2. On 13 September 1939 the Bishop of Leiria "officially made public the devotion of the Five Saturdays revealed by

---

*Paul VI, in the Ecumenical Council—ponder well what this signified— mentioned the consecration made by Pius XII and affirmed that it was an act *not without inspiration from on high;* he then announced that he was sending the Golden Rose to the Sanctuary of Fatima to commemorate this event. (A.A.S. 1964, p. 1017).

the Blessed Virgin to Sister Lucia of Jesus." (*Voice of Fatima,* 13-10-1939). By this act, Dom José Alves Correia da Silva admitted implicitly that the Pontevedra apparitions were not a mere phantasy of the seer.

3. In the notes made by the parish priest of Fatima, Father Manuel Marques Ferreira, on 14 June 1917, we read:

"What do you want of me?"

"I wish you to come here on the 13th and to learn to read so that I can tell you what I want." (*Documentos de Fatima,* p. 500).

Now Lucia, who was not yet attending school, could not learn to read by October 13th, the date of the last apparition in Fatima. If Our Lady told her she must learn to read so that she could tell her what she wanted, it follows that she announced other apparitions later than October 13th.

Why is it, then, that the apparitions of Pontevedra and Tuy are supposed to be the seer's imaginings?

I believe that sufficient reasons have been brought forward for us to admit, without any misgivings, the objectivity of these apparitions and to be able to give our assent to them in the same manner as we do with regard to historical events.

It is unnecessary to repeat that the Church does not propose the Fatima apparitions, or any others, as dogmas of faith. Any person of normal religious culture knows that whatever God intended to reveal to men as truths of faith, that He did, up to the death of the Apostle John. Therefore, the Holy Father emphasized in Fatima that the Church felt that the message imposed a commitment on her *because the appeal of Our Lady is so deeply rooted in the Gospel and the whole of Tradition.*

Guided by these norms, let us begin a closer study of the message.

First Apparition of the Angel

From the very first apparition of the Angel, the responsibility of the members of the Mystical Body in regard to the salvation of souls is heavily underscored.

This is how Sister Lucia describes what happened:

"We had been playing for only a few moments when a strong wind shook the trees and made us raise our eyes to see what was happening, for the day was calm. Then we saw coming towards us, above the olive trees, the figure I have already spoken about. Jacinta and Francisco had never seen it before, nor had I ever talked to them about it. As it drew closer, we were able to distinguish its features. It was a young man, about 14 or 15 years of age, whiter than snow, transparent as crystal when the sun shines through it, and of great beauty. On reaching us, he said, 'Do not be afraid! I am the Angel of Peace. Pray with me.'

"Kneeling on the ground, he bowed down until his forehead touched the ground, and made us repeat these words three times: 'My God, I believe, I adore, I hope and I love You! I ask pardon of You for those who do not believe, do not adore, do not hope and do not love You.' Then, rising, he said, 'Pray thus. The hearts of Jesus and Mary are attentive to the voice of your supplications.'" (*Documentos de Fatima,* pp. 114-116).

The Angel asked the children to pray as he prayed, on bended knees and with forehead touching the ground.

This attitude of reverence before God evokes what St. John describes in the Apocalypse: "The twenty-four elders prostrated themselves before him to worship the One who lives for ever and ever." (*Apoc.* 4:10). "And all the angels who were standing in a circle round the throne, surrounding the elders and the four animals, prostrated themselves before the throne, and touched the ground with their foreheads, worshipping God." (*Apoc.* 7:11). This was the position that Christ took in Gethsemane: "And going on a little further he fell on his face and prayed." (*Matt.* 26:39).

It is sad to see people entering churches or chapels where the Blessed Sacrament is reserved, and seating themselves at once without even making a genuflexion, but crossing their legs as if they had come into a place of entertainment.

Let not the reader think that I defend the proposition that prayer in public must be as the Angel did. *"Est modus in rebus,"* runs the maxim, that is to say, "In everything there is a happy medium."

If from the Angel's posture we pass on to the content of his prayer, we see that it is a prayer of praise to God and of supplication for those who do not believe. Here we have included not only the pagans who do not know the true God, but also the baptized who have unfortunately lost the Faith. "I ask pardon of You for those who do not believe," intimates concern and preoccupation about the salvation of our brothers.

On the other hand, when the Angel assures the children that the hearts of Jesus and Mary are attentive to the voice of their supplications, that is as if it were said: "Your prayers will be heard." Let us have confidence, then, when we pray for the conversion of sinners. "Ask and you shall receive," the divine Master has said.

It is not inappropriate here to recall that the Holy Father, John Paul II, began his homily in the Chapel of the Apparitions with these words: "Praised be our Lord Jesus Christ! And His Mother, Mary Most Holy! Yes, with her and through her there bursts from my heart at this moment the entreaty so often prayed and sung here: 'My God, I believe in You, I adore You, I hope in You, I love You!'"

The Angel said to the little shepherds, "Pray with me"; the Holy Father, in his turn, said, "Pray with Mary and through Mary." We have already seen that Jesus Christ intercedes for us. This means that we are not alone or isolated in our prayers. It is the complete Mystical Body, Head and members, which is praying. That is why the Lord taught us to say "Our Father," and not "My Father." Let us revive our faith! Let us pray with Jesus and with Mary.

"Through Christ, with Christ, in Christ, in the unity of the Holy Spirit, all honour and glory is Yours, Almighty Father, for ever and ever. Amen."

"All these (the Apostles) joined in continuous prayer, together with several women, including Mary the mother of Jesus, and with his brothers." (*Acts* 1:14).

Second and Third Apparitions of the Angel

Sister Lucia thus describes the second apparition of the Angel:

"Some time passed, and summer came, when we had to go home for siesta. One day we were playing on the stone slabs of the well down at the bottom of the garden belonging to my parents, which we called the Arneiro ... Suddenly, we saw beside us the same figure, or rather Angel, as it seemed to me. He said:

'What are you doing? Pray, pray very much! The most holy hearts of Jesus and Mary have designs of mercy on you. Offer prayers and sacrifices constantly to the Most High.'

'How are we to make sacrifices?' I asked.

'Make of everything you can a sacrifice, and offer it to God as an act of reparation for the sins by which He is offended, and in supplication for the conversion of sinners. You will thus draw down peace upon your country. I am its Guardian Angel, the Angel of Portugal. Above all, accept and bear with submission the suffering which the Lord will send you.'" (*Documentos de Fatima,* p. 116).

Here the Angel impresses on the three children the necessity of praying and praying a great deal and adding sacrifices to prayers, to repair the offenses against God, and in supplication for the conversion of sinners. It is, therefore, a repetition of the idea that *in our prayers we should not forget our brothers.*

This responsibility for the salvation of all men should be so taken to heart that we will not be content with simply praying for them, but will be stimulated to offer voluntary sacrifices, or at least to welcome with submission the suffering that the Lord will send us.

It is to our purpose here to quote what Pius XII said in *Mystici Corporis:* "This is a tremendous mystery, and one we cannot sufficiently ponder: The salvation of many souls depends on the prayers and voluntary mortifications of the members of the Mystical Body." Indeed, this truth will be repeatedly borne out in the words spoken by the Mother of God, as we shall see. First, however, it should be noted that in the third apparition of the Angel, besides the emphasis placed on supplication for the conversion of sinners, there is a very significant aspect regarding the offering of reparation which we ought to render to Jesus Christ in the Sacrament of His love for us, which is the Eucharist.

Let us see how Sister Lucia relates the event:

"As soon as we arrived there (some rocks above the Pregueira), we knelt down, with our foreheads touching the ground, and began to repeat the prayer of the Angel: 'My God, I believe, I adore, I hope and I love You . . .' I don't know how many times we had repeated this prayer, when an extraordinary light shone upon us. We sprang up to see what was happening, and beheld the Angel, holding a chalice in his left hand with the Host suspended above it, from which some drops of Blood fell into the chalice. Leaving the chalice suspended in the air, the Angel knelt down beside us and made us repeat three times: 'Most Holy Trinity, Father, Son and Holy Spirit, I offer You the most precious Body, Blood, Soul and Divinity of Jesus Christ, present in all the tabernacles of the world, in reparation for the outrages, sacrileges and indifference with which He Himself is offended. And, through the infinite merits of His most Sacred Heart, and the Immaculate Heart of Mary, I beg of You the conversion of poor sinners.' Then rising, he took the chalice and the Host in his hands. He gave the

Sacred Host to me, and shared the Blood from the chalice between Jacinta and Francisco, saying as he did so, 'Take and drink the Body and Blood of Jesus Christ, horribly outraged by ungrateful men! Make reparation for their crimes and console your God.' Once again, he prostrated on the ground and repeated with us, three times more, the same prayer, 'Most Holy Trinity . . .,' and then disappeared." (*Documentos de Fatima*, p. 118).

A theologian would find difficulty in making a synthesis of such profound teachings in so few words:

—The prayer is Trinitarian.

—It appeals to the infinite merits of the heart of Jesus Christ and of her whom God created Immaculate and made Mother of the Word Incarnate. There is nothing in Heaven or on earth more apt to move God to grant us what we wish to obtain.

—The prayer does not aim at material benefits, but only spiritual ones: the conversion of all sinners, beginning with ourselves, in order to attain the holiness for which we were created.

Apparitions of Our Lady

The apparitions of the Mother of God came to ratify and complete the teachings and recommendations of the Angel and to give them world dimensions, which the first, of themselves, could not obtain.

In 1941, the Bishop of Leiria ordered Sister Lucia to write down an account of the apparitions, and this is what she relates:

"13 May 1917—High up on the slope in the Cova da Iria, I was playing with Jacinta and Francisco at building a little stone wall around a clump of furze. Suddenly we saw what seemed to be a flash of lightning.

'We'd better go home,' I said to my cousins, 'that's lightning; we may have a thunderstorm.'

'Yes indeed!' they answered.

"We began to go down the slope, hurrying the sheep
along towards the road. We were more or less halfway down
the slope, and almost level with a large holm oak tree that
stood there, when we saw another flash of lightning. We
had only gone a few steps further when, there before us on
a small holm oak, we beheld a Lady all dressed in white.
She was more brilliant than the sun, and radiated a light
more clear and intense than a crystal glass filled with
sparkling water, when the rays of the burning sun shine
through it. We stopped, astounded, before the Apparition.
We were so close, just a few feet from her, that we were
bathed in the light which surrounded her, or rather, which
radiated from her. Then Our Lady spoke to us:

'Do not be afraid. I will do you no harm.'

'Where are you from?'

'I am from Heaven.'

'What do you want of me?'

'I have come to ask you to come here for six months in
succession, on the 13th day, at this same hour. Later on, I
will tell you who I am and what I want. Afterwards, I will
return here yet a seventh time.'

'Shall I go to Heaven too?'

'Yes, you will.'

'And Jacinta?'

'She will go also.'

'And Francisco?'

'He will go there too, but he must say many Rosaries.'

"Then I remembered to ask about two girls who had died
recently. They were friends of mine and used to come to my
home to learn weaving with my eldest sister.

'Is Maria das Neves in Heaven?'

'Yes, she is.' (I think she was about 16 years old).

'And Amélia?'

'She will be in Purgatory until the end of the world.'* (It seems to me that she was between 18 and 20 years of age).

'Are you willing to offer yourselves to God and to bear all the sufferings He wills to send you, as an act of reparation for the sins by which He is offended, and of supplication for the conversion of sinners?'

'Yes, we are willing.'

'Then you are going to have much to suffer, but the grace of God will be your comfort.'

"As she pronounced these last words, 'the grace of God will be your comfort,' Our Lady opened her hands for the first time, communicating to us a light so intense that, as it streamed from her hands, its rays penetrated our hearts and the innermost depths of our souls, making us see ourselves in God, who was that light, more clearly than we see ourselves in the best of mirrors. Then moved by an interior impulse that was also communicated to us, we fell on our knees, repeating in our hearts, 'O most Holy Trinity, I adore You! My God, my God, I love You in the most Blessed Sacrament!' After a few moments, Our Lady spoke again: 'Pray the Rosary every day, in order to obtain peace for the world and the end of the war.'" (*Documentos de Fatima*, pp. 328-332).

From this simple and unpretentious account of one who wrote offhand, with no time for rough notes or corrections, what stands out is the need for **prayer** and **reparation** for sins, one's own and those of others. Francisco will indeed go to Heaven, but first he must pray *many* Rosaries. Amélia must undergo in Purgatory the reparation which she failed to make in this world.

The Portuguese Bishops, in their pastoral instruction

---

*Our Lady's statement admits of a conditional interpretation, such as we learn from the Book of Jonas, Exodus 32:10, and the Prophet Jeremiah 18:7. Amélia will be in Purgatory until the end of the world if there is no one to pray for her, or have Holy Mass offered for her, just as "many souls go to Hell, because there are none to sacrifice themselves and to pray for them."

about discipline, quoted this passage of Paul VI: "We have sinned, we have contracted a debt. For there exists an objective order of justice and the just God proposes a law to us, a law of demanding love; and if we have not observed it, we must give an account to the Lord. It is fitting then, to return to that discipline which seeks to welcome divine justice and makes us kneel before God, ready to assume any punishment in order to be spared more serious penalties." (*Lumen,* Feb. 1982, pp. 54-55).

The Mother of Mercy, therefore, makes a motherly appeal to the generosity of the three innocent children, that they offer to God their suffering—which will come from their families or other persons—as an act of reparation and of supplication for the conversion of sinners.

But in this same apparition, there is another teaching, which up to the present has not been mentioned in many works about Fatima. Our Lady spoke to the children of sufferings which *God wished to send them.* Now the little shepherds were indeed to have much to suffer, owing to the incredulity of members of their families and of those who accounted them as deceivers. There were priests who tortured them with endless interrogations, to such an extent that Sister Lucia wrote: "On one occasion, a priest from Torres Novas came to question me. When he did so, he went into such minute details, and tried so hard to trip me up, that afterwards I felt some scruples about having concealed certain things from him. I consulted my cousins on the matter:

'I don't know,' I asked them, 'if we are doing wrong by not telling everything, when they ask us if Our Lady told us anything else. When we just say that she told us a secret, I don't know whether we are lying or not, by saying nothing about the rest.'

'I don't know,' replied Jacinta, 'that's up to you! You're the one who does not want us to say anything.'

'Of course I don't want you to say anything,' I answered. 'Why, they'll start asking what sort of mortifications we are practising! And that would be the last straw!'

"A little while later, another priest appeared; he was from Santarém. He looked like a brother of the first I've just spoken of, or at least they seemed to have rehearsed things together, asking the same questions, making the same attempts to trip me up, laughing and making fun of me in the same way; in fact their very height and features were almost identical. After this interrogation, my doubt was stronger than ever, and I really did not know what course of action to follow. I constantly pleaded with Our Lord and Our Lady to tell me what to do. 'O my God, and my dearest Mother in Heaven, you know that I do not want to offend You by telling lies; but You are well aware that it would not be right to tell them all that You told me!'" (*Documentos de Fatima,* pp. 168-170).

But the most inhuman psychological torture came to them from the Administrator of Vila Nova de Ourém. There, they were threatened with death in a cauldron of boiling oil, if they did not tell the Secret.

Now, all these sufferings came to them from men and not directly from God. Here then is confirmed what I have stated hitherto, that is, that God acts always by means of secondary causes. Nothing happens in this world without His permission or consent. It is Jesus Christ Himself who so teaches us: "Can you not buy five sparrows for two pennies? And yet not one is forgotten in God's sight. Why, every hair on your head has been counted. There is no need to be afraid: you are worth more than hundreds of sparrows." (*Lk.* 12:6-7).

Spiritual Purity

Through an attentive reading of the seer's writings, one can discover in them a characteristic sign of true communications with the supernatural world: humility, or spiritual purity. Truly, the little Lucia, only ten years old, was tortured by scruples of doubt "as to whether she was lying" by concealing the Lady's request to make sacrifices.

This concern about hiding from the public, including her own parents, the heroic sacrifices which they practised, was shared also with Jacinta and Francisco:

"Around that time,* Jacinta and Francisco also began to grow worse. Jacinta used to tell me sometimes, 'My chest hurts so much, but I'm not saying anything to my mother! I want to suffer for Our Lord, in reparation for the sins committed against the Immaculate Heart of Mary, for the Holy Father and for the conversion of sinners.' One morning, when I went to see her, she asked me:

'How many sacrifices did you offer to Our Lord last night?'

'Three. I got up three times to recite the Angel's prayers.'

'Well, I offered Him many, many sacrifices. I don't know how many there were, but I had a lot of pain, and I made no complaint.'

"Francisco spoke very little. He usually did everything he saw us doing, and rarely suggested anything himself. During his illness, he suffered with heroic patience, without ever letting the slightest moan or the least complaint escape his lips. One day, shortly before his death, I asked him, 'Are you suffering a lot, Francisco?'

'Yes, but I suffer it all for love of Our Lord and Our Lady.'

"One day, he gave me the rope that I have already spoken about, saying, 'Take it away before my mother sees it. I don't feel able to wear it any more around my waist.'

"He took everything his mother offered him, and she could never discover which things he disliked." (*Documentos de Fatima,* p. 194).

---

*Jacinta and Francisco fell ill with the Spanish influenza epidemic towards the end of 1918, and were confined to bed on 23-12-1918. (cf. Visconde de Montello, *Fatima Happenings,* Guarda 1923, pp. 18-19).

Jacinta's habit of concealing her sufferings is referred to in other documents which, as I understand, are still unpublished.

The head nurse of Unit 5 of D. Estefânia Hospital in 1920, Luísa da Conceição Ribeiro, declared to Sister Maria do Carmo Lopes de Fonseca, who on 25 May 1957 began an enquiry in Lisbon about Jacinta:

"She was brought to the hospital by some ladies. At the time I had not the slightest idea that she was the seer of Fatima. She came in there like any young girl. She was very ill indeed. She had an opening in the chest. By nature she was very quiet. She never complained but only moaned, and spoke very little." (*Formigão Archives,* P 7, 24, p. 12).

In her enquiry, Sr. Maria do Carmo recorded the evidence of two nurses, who had treated Jacinta in the above-mentioned hospital. She writes thus regarding an interview with Maria do Rosário Santos Rego:

"In her daily rounds of the wards she passed through Unit 5 as well. Now it happened that Jacinta began to attract her attention by the manner in which she looked at her and the way her eyes followed her about. All during the time she remained in the ward until she left by the terrace door, Jacinta kept her eyes fixed on her. The recollection of that look, therefore, was indelibly stamped on her memory. 'That child had such beautiful eyes!' she said.

"Sometimes she greeted Jacinta, but the seer spoke little and with effort. She therefore avoided tiring her. Yet she could see that the child was different from the others. So very patient . . . a little saint! She never heard her cry out, and she never saw her angry. And the former staff nurse repeated, 'Yes, she was different from the others in everything.'" (*Ib.,* pp. 10-11).

To conclude, let us hear the evidence of Leonor Assunção de Almeida:

"'What impressions do you retain about Jacinta?'

'She was a very quiet child, and she never complained! . . . She spoke little and seemed very introspective.

She prayed a great deal and continually called on Our Lady
in her sufferings.'" (*Ib.,* pp. 13-14).

July and August Apparitions

Let us return to the Fourth Memoir in which Sister
Lucia, by order of the Bishop of Leiria, related the history
of the apparitions of 1917:

"13 July 1917—A few moments after arriving at the
Cova da Iria, near the holm oak, where a large number of
people were praying the Rosary, we saw the flash of light
once more, and a moment later Our Lady appeared on the
holm oak.

'What do you want of me?' I asked.

'I want you to come here on the 13th of next month, to
continue to pray the Rosary every day in honour of Our
Lady of the Rosary, in order to obtain peace for the world
and the end of the war, because only she can help you.'

'I would like to ask you to tell us who you are, and to
work a miracle so that everybody will believe that you are
appearing to us.'

'Continue to come here every month. In October, I will
tell you who I am and what I want, and I will perform a
miracle for all to see and believe.'

"I then made some requests, but I cannot recall now just
what they were. What I do remember is that Our Lady said
it was necessary for such people to pray the Rosary in order
to obtain these graces during the year. And she continued,
'Sacrifice yourselves for sinners, and say many times,
especially whenever you make some sacrifice: O Jesus, it is
for love of You, for the conversion of sinners, and in
reparation for the sins committed against the Immaculate
Heart of Mary.'

"As Our Lady spoke these last words, she opened her
hands once more, as she had done during the two previous

months. The rays of light seemed to penetrate the earth, and we saw, as it were, a sea of fire. Plunged in this fire were demons and souls in human form, like transparent burning embers, all blackened or burnished bronze, floating about in the conflagration, now raised into the air by the flames that issued from within themselves together with great clouds of smoke, now falling back on every side like sparks in huge fires, without weight or equilibrium, amid shrieks and groans of pain and despair, which horrified us and made us tremble with fear. (It must have been this sight which caused me to cry out, as people say they heard me). The demons could be distinguished by their terrifying and repellent likeness to frightful and unknown animals, black and transparent like burning coals.

"Terrified and as if to plead for succour, we looked up at Our Lady, who said to us, so kindly and so sadly, 'You have seen Hell where the souls of poor sinners go. To save them, God wishes to establish in the world devotion to my Immaculate Heart. If what I say to you is done, many souls will be saved and there will be peace. The war is going to end; but if people do not cease offending God, a worse one will break out during the pontificate of Pius XI. When you see a night illumined by an unknown light, know that this is the great sign given you by God that He is about to punish the world for its crimes, by means of war, famine, and persecutions of the Church and of the Holy Father.

'To prevent this, I shall come to ask for the consecration of Russia to my Immaculate Heart, and the Communion of Reparation on the First Saturdays. If my requests are heeded, Russia will be converted, and there will be peace. If not, she will spread her errors throughout the world, causing wars and persecutions of the Church. The good will be martyred, the Holy Father will have much to suffer, various nations will be annihilated. In the end my Immaculate Heart will triumph. The Holy Father will consecrate Russia to me, and she will be converted, and a period of peace will be granted to the world. In Portugal, the dogma of the Faith will always be preserved; etc. . . . Do not tell this to anybody. Francisco, yes, you may tell him.'

"13 August 1917—As I have already said what happened on this day, I will not delay over it here, but pass on to the apparition which, in my opinion, took place on the 15th in the afternoon. As at that time I did not yet know how to reckon the days of the month, it could be that I am mistaken. But I still have an idea that it took place on the very day that we arrived back from Vila Nova de Ourém.

"I was accompanied by Francisco and his brother John. We were with the sheep in a place called Valinhos, when we felt something supernatural approaching and enveloping us. Suspecting that Our Lady was about to appear to us, and feeling sorry lest Jacinta might miss seeing her, we asked her brother John to go and call her. As he was unwilling to go, I offered him two small coins, and off he ran.

"Meanwhile, Francisco and I saw the flash of light, which we called lightning. Jacinta arrived, and a moment later, we saw Our Lady on a holm oak tree.

'What do you want of me?'

'I want you to continue going to the Cova da Iria on the 13th, and to continue praying the Rosary every day. In the last month, I will perform a miracle so that all may believe.'

'What do you want done with the money that the people leave in the Cova da Iria?'

'Have two litters made. One is to be carried by you and Jacinta and two other girls dressed in white, the other one is to be carried by Francisco and three other boys. The money from the litters is for the "festa" of Our Lady of the Rosary; and what is left over will help towards the construction of a chapel that is to be built.'

'I would like to ask you to cure some sick persons.'

'Yes, I will cure some of them during the year.'

"And then looking very sad, she said, 'Pray, pray very much, and make sacrifices for sinners; for many souls go to Hell, because there are none to sacrifice themselves and to pray for them.' And she began to ascend as usual towards the east." (*Documentos de Fatima,* pp. 336-344).

It is in these two apparitions that our responsibility in regard to the salvation of our brothers shines with a more intense light. Our Lady could not be more categorical and emphatic: **Pray, pray very much, and make sacrifices for sinners; for many souls go to Hell, because there are none to sacrifice themselves and to pray for them.**

This phrase of profound theological meaning has provoked qualms among some priests, in Portugal and abroad.* Thank God, they are the exception. The more discerning, an overwhelming majority, see in it a loving admonition of the Mother of God and of the Church, which serves to rouse us from our egoistic slumber to the divine reality of belonging to the Mystical Body of Christ.

There is an intimate and mysterious union between the Head and the members, between the Vine and the branches: "I am the vine, you are the branches." (*Jn.* 15:5).

That is why St. Paul reasoned with the Christians of Corinth: "You know, surely, that your bodies are members making up the body of Christ; do you think I can take parts of Christ's body and join them to the body of a prostitute? *God forbid! Never!* As you know, a man who goes with a prostitute is one body with her, since the two, as it is said, become one flesh. But anyone who is joined to the Lord is one spirit with him." (*1 Cor.* 6:15-17). And in writing to the Galatians he said to them, "There are no more distinctions between Jew and Greek, slave and free, male and female, but *all of you are one in Christ Jesus."* (*Gal.* 3:28).

The Body of Christ is the Church, as St. Paul declares: "It makes me happy to suffer for you, as I am suffering now, and in my own body to do what I can to make up all that has still to be undergone by Christ for the sake of his body, the Church." (*Col.* 1:24).

But what is the meaning which we should attribute to the

---

*I have replied to two of them in *Documentos de Fatima,* pp. 527-528, and in the review *Magnificat,* March-April 1981.

Apostle's words?

Certainly he did not intend to affirm that the sufferings of Christ were insufficient towards redeeming all mankind, for the reparation given to the Father by the Son of God, by reason of the Hypostatic union, has infinite value and has no need of completion. St. Paul's thought ought to be understood, therefore, in the sense that, the Church being the Body of Christ, each Christian must be associated with the Head in the work of reconciliation or redemption. It is something similar to the mystery of the bloody sacrifice of the cross which should be renewed in an unbloody manner in the Mass until the end of the world.

It is for this reason that Pius XI states in his encyclical *Miserentissimus Redemptor* of 8 May, 1928: "So it is that the expiatory Passion of Christ is renewed and in a certain manner continued and filled up in His Mystical Body which is the Church. For, to quote St. Augustine again, 'Christ suffered all that He had to suffer; now nothing is lacking to the measure of His sufferings. But the sufferings have been completed only for the Head; there still remain the sufferings of Christ's body.' (*On Ps.* 86).

"This truth Christ Himself deigned to express when He said to Saul, who was 'as yet breathing out threatenings and slaughter against the disciples' (*Acts* 9:1), 'I am Jesus, whom thou persecutest' (*Acts* 9:5), signifying clearly that when persecution is unleashed against the Church, the Divine Head of the Church is opposed and harassed. It is therefore only right that Christ, who suffers still in His Mystical Body, should wish to have us associates of His expiation. Our very relationship with Him even requires it; for since we are 'the body of Christ and members of member' (*1 Cor.* 12:27), whatever the Head suffers, all the members should suffer with Him."

Our Lady not only reminded us of the responsibility we have in the salvation of our brothers, but like a good teacher, she summarized it in two brief formulas of prayer—one to be prayed between each Mystery of the

Rosary: "O my Jesus, forgive us, save us from the fire of Hell. Lead all souls to Heaven, especially those who are most in need." (*Documentos de Fatima,* pp. 340-342). Here it is opportune to point out that this prayer is yet another proof of who was really appearing to the children, that it was the Mother of God. For the three little shepherds were incapable of inventing such a prayer, which was not prayed anywhere. The other prayer was to be said *many times,* in particular when making a sacrifice: "O Jesus, it is for love of You, for the conversion of sinners, and in reparation for the sins committed against the Immaculate Heart of Mary." (*Documentos de Fatima,* p. 338).

How the crude habits of many persons would change if, instead of giving vent to coarse language whenever something disagreeable happens to them, they would accustom themselves to pray this prayer taught by Our Lady to the little shepherds! They would be doing no more than taking St. Paul's advice: "Guard against foul talk; let your words be for the improvement of others, as occasion offers, and do good to your listeners, otherwise you will only be grieving the Holy Spirit of God who has marked you with his seal for you to be set free when the day of redemption comes." (*Eph.* 4:29-30).

The seers absorbed admirably the teachings of the Mother of God. They patiently accepted every suffering, offering it to the Lord through this prayer taught by the Most Holy Virgin, as we have seen in the case of being abandoned by their parents when they were imprisoned in Vila Nova de Ourém.

But there are other points to consider in the July apparition.

When Lucia presented to Our Lady the requests which had been confided to her, she replied that *it was necessary to pray the Rosary* to obtain these graces during the year. So here we have a fresh insistence on the need for prayer and that, as an indispensable condition, it is required in order to obtain the desired favours.

Having said this, it is time to approach the subject which
has aroused the greatest attention in the writings of the seer:
the vision of Hell.

The Vision of Hell

What is to be thought about this description by Sister
Lucia?

Before all else, it should be borne in mind that in the
supernatural sphere it is one thing to have contemplated or
felt the realities of the hereafter, and another the possibility
of describing them.

St. Paul gives us this vivid passage regarding his visions:
"I know a man in Christ who, fourteen years ago, was
caught up—whether still in the body or out of the body, I
do not know; God knows—right into the third heaven. I do
know, however, that this same person—whether in the body
or out of the body, I do not know; God knows—was caught
up into paradise and heard things which must not and cannot be put into human language." (*2 Cor.* 12:2-4).

The reality of Hell is a mystery that is incomprehensible*

---

*Perhaps it would be less incomprehensible if we were to pay attention
to the psychological reality of the guilty who are led to flee from the
persons whom they have offended. Genesis interprets this natural senti-
ment, saying that Adam and Eve, after their disobedience, "hid themselves from the face of the Lord God." (*Gen.* 3:8).

It is not necessary for God to condemn anyone to Hell. The soul in
grave sin, of itself flees from the all-holy God. Judas, after his crime,
committed suicide. The newspapers referred recently to a child of
twelve years who, having stolen a small sum of money and seeing himself discovered, put an end to his own life.

What will be the sentiments of those who, after death, see very
clearly their folly in this life by preferring to love themselves and other
creatures selfishly rather than loving God, who is Infinite Love?
Moreover, it happens that people who allow themselves to be drawn
away by vices greatly dislike to be told: "You are a thief, a murderer, a
perverter." If, here on earth, vices called by their proper name cause
shame, what will it be like before God, face to face?

to our sensibility, but it is equally a truth of faith which the Catholic Church has always defended through the ages.

This is how two eminent theologians explain it:

"The Ecclesiastical Magisterium declares that Hell exists (*Dz.* 16, 40, 429, 464, 714), that punishment follows immediately after death (and not only after the Last Judgement) and that it is eternal. (*Dz.* 531, 211).

"Without fear of being mistaken, we must profess jointly the doctrine of the force of a universal salvific will of God and of the real possibility of eternal damnation." (K. Rahner-H. Vorgrimler, *Diccionario Teologica,* Barcelona 1966, p. 432).

The authors quoted have based their statements on documents which are inaccessible to the majority of readers. Therefore, I am inserting them here:

Dz. 40 is an extract from the Quicumque Creed, which says: "Whoever wishes to be saved must, above all, keep the Catholic Faith; for unless a person keeps this Faith whole and entire, he will undoubtedly be lost forever. . . . Christ . . . sits at the right hand of God the Father almighty, and from there He shall come to judge the living and the dead. At His coming all men are to arise with their own bodies; and they are to give an account of their lives. Those who have done good deeds will go into eternal life; those who have done evil will go into everlasting fire."

Dz. 429 reproduces an excerpt from the Fourth Lateran Council, which was the twelfth Ecumenical Council and which, in its definition against the Albigenses and other heretics, professes:

"Jesus Christ, the only-begotten Son of God . . . will come at the end of the world; He will judge the living and the dead; and He will reward all, both the lost and the elect, according to their works. And all these will rise with their own bodies which they now have so that they may receive according to their works, whether good or bad; the wicked, a perpetual punishment with the devil; the good, eternal glory with Christ."

The Church, in these professions of faith, does no more than adhere to the teachings of Jesus Christ and the Apostles, which refer repeatedly to the eternal punishment destined for those who obstinately refuse the infinite love of the Father.

In order to describe this punishment, expressions like these are used: "a blazing furnace where there will be weeping and grinding of teeth" (*Mt.* 13:42-50); "eternal fire" (*Mt.* 18:9); "eternal punishment" (*Mt.* 25:46 and *2 Th.* 1:9); and a "burning lake of sulphur" (*Apoc.* 21:8).

Nevertheless, these expressions are simply means to explain a reality which is not of this world, but of what is beyond, and consequently they are untransmissible by human language.

This is what must be kept in mind when considering the description given by Sister Lucia. The vision of Hell was a mystical grace granted to the three little shepherds, which the seer transmitted as well as she could. It is useless to press the matter further, as for example to investigate if this description is the fruit of readings and sermons heard in infancy.

The biblical authors, in spite of being inspired by God, wrote in accordance with the scientific knowledge which each of them possessed. Therefore, we come across passages in the Sacred Books like this: "And the sun stood still, and the moon halted, till the people had vengeance on their enemies." (*Jos.* 10:13).

The conclusion is evident: In the biblical books, as in those which transmit mystical communications, we must not dwell on an analysis of the phrases in themselves, but on that which God, through this means, wishes to communicate to us.

Now, in the case of Fatima, the vision of Hell impelled the three children to make truly heroic acts for the conversion of sinners. More than a dozen pages would be needed to transcribe all the sacrifices narrated in the four Memoirs. Here are some examples:

"Jacinta took this matter of making sacrifices for the conversion of sinners so much to heart, that she never let a single opportunity escape her. There were two families in Moita whose children used to go round begging from door to door. We met them one day as we were going along with our sheep. As soon as she saw them, Jacinta said to us: 'Let's give our lunch to those poor children, for the conversion of sinners.' And she ran to take it to them.

"That afternoon, she told me she was hungry. There were holm oaks and oak trees nearby. The acorns were still quite green. However, I told her we could eat them. Francisco climbed up a holm oak to fill his pockets, but Jacinta remembered that we could eat the ones on the oak trees instead, and thus make a sacrifice by eating the bitter kind. So it was there, that afternoon, that we enjoyed this delicious repast! Jacinta made this one of her usual sacrifices, and often picked the acorns off the oaks or the olives off the trees. One day I said to her:

'Jacinta, don't eat that; it's too bitter!'

'But it's because it's bitter that I'm eating it, for the conversion of sinners.'

"These were not the only times we fasted. We had agreed that whenever we met any poor children like these, we would give them our lunch. They were only too happy to receive such an alms, and they took good care to meet us; they used to wait for us along the road. We no sooner saw them than Jacinta ran to give them all the food we had for the day, as happy as if she had no need of it herself. On days like that, our only nourishment consisted of pine nuts, and little berries about the size of an olive which grow on the roots of yellow bellflowers, as well as blackberries, mushrooms, and some other things we found on the roots of pine trees—I can't remember now what these were called.* If there was fruit available on the land belonging to our

---

*They are called "putegas" or "coalhadas," an edible plant of the rafflesia family.

parents, we used to eat that.

"Jacinta's thirst for making sacrifices seemed insatiable. One day a neighbour offered my mother a good pasture for our sheep. Though it was quite far away and we were at the height of summer, my mother accepted the offer made so generously, and sent me there. She told me that we should take our siesta in the shade of the trees, as there was a pond nearby where the flock could go and drink. On the way, we met our dear poor children, and Jacinta ran to give them our usual alms. It was a lovely day, but the sun was blazing, and in that arid, stony wasteland, it seemed as though it would burn everything up. We were parched with thirst, and there wasn't a single drop of water for us to drink! At first, we offered the sacrifice generously for the conversion of sinners, but after midday we could hold out no longer.

"As there was a house quite near, I suggested to my companions that I should go and ask for a little water. They agreed to this, so I went and knocked on the door. A little old woman gave me not only a pitcher of water, but also some bread, which I accepted gratefully. I ran to share it with my little companions, and then offered the pitcher to Francisco, and told him to take a drink.

'I don't want to,' he replied.

'Why?'

'I want to suffer for the conversion of sinners.'

'You have a drink, Jacinta!'

'But I want to offer this sacrifice for sinners, too.'

"Then I poured the water into a hollow in the rock, so that the sheep could drink it, and went to return the pitcher to its owner. The heat was getting more and more intense. The shrill singing of the crickets and grasshoppers coupled with the croaking of the frogs in the neighbouring pond made an uproar that was almost unbearable. Jacinta, frail as she was, and weakened still more by the lack of food and drink, said to me with that simplicity which was natural to her:

'Tell the crickets and the frogs to keep quiet! I have such

a terrible headache.'

"Then Francisco asked her, 'Don't you want to suffer this for sinners?'

"The poor child, clasping her head between her two little hands, replied, 'Yes. I do. Let them sing!'" (*Documentos de Fatima*, pp. 38-42).

"We were playing one day at the well I have already mentioned. Close to it, there was a grapevine belonging to Jacinta's mother. She cut a few clusters and brought them to us to eat. But Jacinta never forgot her sinners.

'We won't eat them,' she said, 'we'll offer this sacrifice for sinners.'

"Then she ran out with the grapes and gave them to the other children playing on the road. She returned radiant with joy, for she had found our poor children, and given them the grapes.

"Another time, my aunt called us to come and eat some figs which she had brought home, and indeed they would have given anybody an appetite. Jacinta sat down happily next to the basket, with the rest of us, and picked up the first fig. She was just about to eat it, when she suddenly remembered, and said, 'It's true! Today we haven't yet made a single sacrifice for sinners! We'll have to make this one.'

"She put the fig back in the basket, and made the offering; and we, too, left our figs in the basket for the conversion of sinners. Jacinta made such sacrifices over and over again, but I won't stop to tell any more, or I shall never end." (*Documentos de Fatima*, p. 66).

One must needs be profoundly convinced that the salvation of souls depends on our prayers and sacrifices, united to the prayers and holocaust of the divine Victim of Calvary, to attain the heroism revealed in these pages just quoted. Through them it is clear that the children, moved undoubtedly by the Holy Spirit, captured instinctively the biblical meaning of the forms of penance: fasting and prayer.

Actually, passages like these abound in Sacred Scripture:
"And Eliachim, the Lord's high priest, went about everywhere among the Israelite folk with words of comfort: 'Be
sure,' he said, 'that the Lord will listen to your plea, if you
pray on, fast on in his presence.'" (*Judith* 4:10-12).

King David, referring to those who persecuted him,
affirmed in *Ps.* 34:13: "When they were troublesome to me,
I humbled my soul with fasting."

In the New Testament we have the shining example of
Jesus as well as that of John the Baptist. The latter not only
fasted but encouraged his disciples to do the same, so that
they wondered why those who followed the Lord did not do
likewise: "Then John's disciples came to him (Our Lord)
and said, 'Why is it that we and the Pharisees fast, but your
disciples do not?' Jesus replied, 'Surely the bridegroom's at-
tendants would never think of mourning as long as the
bridegroom is still with them? But the time will come for
the bridegroom to be taken away from them, and then they
will fast.'" (*Mt.* 9:14-15).

At that time Jesus defended His own disciples, but on
another occasion He let them know that prayer and fasting
are indispensable means to overcome evil spirits: "There is
no way of casting out such spirits as this except by prayer
and fasting." (*Mt.* 17:22).

As regards almsgiving, the book of Tobit recommends:
"Set aside part of your goods for almsgiving. Never turn
your face from any poor man and God will never turn his
from you ... Alms is a most effective offering for all those
who give it in the presence of the Most High." (*Tob.*
4:7-11). "Prayer with fasting and alms with right conduct
are better than riches with iniquity. Better to practise
almsgiving than to hoard up gold. Almsgiving saves from
death and purges every kind of sin." (*Tob.* 12:8-9).

And Jesus Christ counsels: "Sell your possessions and
give alms. Get yourselves purses that do not wear out, treas-

ure that will not fail you, in heaven where no thief can reach it and no moth destroy it. For where your treasure is, there will your heart be also." (*Lk.* 12:33-34).*

Jacinta's Treasure

Jacinta's treasure lay in her ardour to save all sinners. The mystic grace of the vision of Hell had impressed her so vividly that she did not lose a single opportunity to offer sacrifices to God for the conversion of the prodigal sons. It even seemed to her that if Our Lady showed Hell to everybody it would be an infallible remedy for abandoning sin. This is what Lucia tells us:

"Jacinta often sat thoughtfully on the ground or on a rock, and exclaimed, 'Oh, Hell! Hell! How sorry I am for the souls who go to Hell! And the people down there, burning alive, like wood in the fire!' Then, shuddering, she knelt down with her hands joined, and recited the prayer that Our Lady had taught us: 'O my Jesus! Forgive us, save us from the fire of Hell. Lead all souls to Heaven, especially those who are most in need.' She remained on her knees like this for long periods of time, saying the same prayer over and over again. From time to time, like someone awaking from sleep, she called out to her brother or myself, 'Francisco! Francisco! Are you praying with me? We must pray, very much, to save souls from Hell! So many go there! So many!'

---

*However, in giving alms, it should be discovered that he who asks is truly in need. Unfortunately, there are numerous false beggars to be found everywhere, who do not wish to work, to whom St. Paul's words would well apply: "not to let anyone have any food if he refused to do any work." (*2 Th.* 3:10). To aid the truly indigent, several specialized organizations have been set up, such as the St. Vincent de Paul confraternities, Caritas International, which has its branches in nearly every country, the Red Cross, Mother Teresa of Calcutta's works of mercy, etc. Through these bodies, relief can be brought to thousands of persons in danger of death through malnutrition and the dreadful suffering of hunger.

At other times she asked, 'Why doesn't Our Lady show Hell to sinners? If they saw it they would not sin, so as to avoid going there! You must tell Our Lady to show Hell to all the people (referring to those who were in the Cova da Iria at the time of the apparition). You'll see how they will be converted.' Afterwards, unsatisfied, she asked me, 'Why didn't you tell Our Lady to show Hell to those people?'

'I forgot,' I answered.

'I didn't remember either!' she said, looking very sad.

"Sometimes she also asked, 'What are the sins people commit, for which they go to Hell?'

'I don't know! Perhaps the sin of not going to Mass on Sunday, of stealing, of saying ugly words, of cursing and swearing.'

'So for just one word, then, people can go to Hell?'

'Well, it's a sin!'

'It wouldn't be hard for them to keep quiet, and to go to Mass! I'm so sorry for sinners! If only I could show them Hell!'

"Suddenly, she would seize hold of me and say:

'I'm going to Heaven, but you are staying here. If Our Lady lets you, tell everybody what Hell is like, so that they won't commit any more sins and won't go to Hell.'

"At other times, after thinking for a while, she said, 'So many people falling into Hell! So many people in Hell!' To quieten her I said, 'Don't be afraid! You're going to Heaven.' 'Yes, I am,' she said serenely, 'but I want all those people to go there too!'

"When, in a spirit of mortification, she did not want to eat, I said to her, 'Jacinta! Come and eat now.'

'No! I'm offering this sacrifice for sinners who eat too much.'

"When she was ill, and yet went to Mass on a weekday, I urged her:

'Jacinta, don't come! You can't, you're not able. Besides, today is not a Sunday!'

'That doesn't matter! I'm going for sinners who don't go

on a Sunday!'" (*Documentos de Fatima,* pp. 220-224).

What an admirable spirit of reparation was that of the little Jacinta—to make the sacrifice, even when ill, of going to Mass on weekdays to make up for those who do not even go on Sundays—and there are so many! Here is the opportune time to ask: What will those Christians respond to Jesus Christ, on the day of judgement, who for futile reasons missed Mass, or what will be their answer when the divine Judge questions them in these or similar words: "The week has ten thousand and eighty minutes; could you not have found sixty minutes to assist at the Holy Sacrifice, the memorial of My Passion, in which I shed all My Blood for you? How did you use your time?"

These are burning questions, tremendously embarrassing! The reply must inevitably be that which we find in the book of Wisdom: "We have crossed deserts where there was no track, but the way of the Lord is one we have never known. Arrogance, what advantage has this brought us? Wealth and boasting, what have these conferred on us? All those things have passed like a shadow." (*Wis.* 5:7-9).

In order to avoid an error so tragic and fatal, it is very salutary to reflect on eternity from time to time, as Jacinta did. This reflection could lead even good Christians, as well as priests and religious, to discover that it is very easy to lose precious time in useless things.

September and October Apparitions

But let us return to Sister Lucia's account, in which she relates to us the last two apparitions in the Cova da Iria:

"13 September 1917—As the hour approached, I set out with Jacinta and Francisco, but owing to the crowds around us we could only advance with difficulty. The roads were packed with people ... At last, we arrived at the Cova da Iria, and on reaching the holm oak we began to say the

Rosary with the people. Shortly afterward, we saw the flash of light, and then Our Lady appeared on the holm oak.

'Continue to pray the Rosary in order to obtain the end of the war. In October Our Lord will come, as well as Our Lady of Dolours and Our Lady of Carmel. St. Joseph will appear with the Child Jesus to bless the world. God is pleased with your sacrifices. He does not want you to sleep with the rope on, but only to wear it during the daytime.'

'I was told to ask you for many things, the cure of some sick people, of a deaf-mute . . .'

'Yes, I will cure some, but not others. In October I will perform a miracle so that all may believe.'

"Then Our Lady began to rise as usual, and disappeared.

"13 October 1917—We left home quite early, expecting that we would be delayed along the way. Masses of people thronged the roads. The rain fell in torrents. My mother, her heart torn with uncertainty as to what was going to happen, and fearing it would be the last day of my life, wanted to accompany me. On the way, the scenes of the previous month, still more numerous and moving, were repeated. Not even the muddy roads could prevent these people from kneeling in the most humble and suppliant of attitudes. We reached the holm oak in the Cova da Iria. Once there, moved by an interior impulse, I asked the people to shut their umbrellas and say the Rosary. A little later, we saw the flash of light, and then Our Lady appeared on the holm oak.

'What do you want of me?'

'I want to tell you that a chapel is to be built here in my honour. I am the Lady of the Rosary. Continue always to pray the Rosary every day. The war is going to end, and the soldiers will soon return to their homes.'

'I have many things to ask you: the cure of some sick persons, the conversion of sinners, and other things . . .'

'Some yes, but not others. They must amend their lives and ask forgiveness for their sins.' Looking very sad, Our Lady said, 'Do not offend the Lord our God any more, because He is already so much offended.'

"Then, opening her hands, she made them reflect on the sun, and as she ascended, the reflection of her own light continued to be projected on the sun itself.

"Here, Your Excellency, is the reason why I cried out to the people to look at the sun. My aim was not to call their attention to the sun, because I was not even aware of their presence. I was moved to do so under the guidance of an interior impulse.

"After Our Lady had disappeared into the immense distance of the firmament, we beheld St. Joseph with the Child Jesus and Our Lady robed in white with a blue mantle, beside the sun. St. Joseph and the Child Jesus appeared to bless the world, for they traced the Sign of the Cross with their hands. When, a little later, this apparition disappeared, I saw Our Lord and Our Lady; it seemed to me that it was Our Lady of Dolours. Our Lord appeared to bless the world in the same manner as St. Joseph had done. This apparition also vanished, and I saw Our Lady once more, this time resembling Our Lady of Carmel.

"Here then, Your Excellency, you have the story of the apparitions of Our Lady in the Cova da Iria, in 1917. Whenever and for whatever motive I had to speak of them, I sought to do so in as few words as possible, with the desire of keeping to myself alone those more intimate aspects which were so difficult for me to reveal. But as they belong to God and not to me, here they are. I return what does not belong to me. To the best of my knowledge, I keep nothing back. I think I have only omitted some minor details referring to the petitions which I made. As these were merely material things, I did not attach such great importance to them, and it is perhaps because of this that they did not make such a vivid impression on my mind; and then there were so many of them, so very many! It was possibly because I was so anxious to remember the innumerable graces that I had to ask Our Lady that I was mistaken when I understood that the war would end on that very 13th.

"Not a few people have expressed considerable surprise at the memory that God has deigned to give me. In this matter indeed I have, through His infinite goodness, been quite favoured in every respect. Where supernatural things are concerned, this is not to be wondered at, for these are imprinted on the mind in such a way that it is almost impossible to forget them. At least, the meaning of what is made known is never forgotten, unless it be that God also wills that this too be forgotten." (*Documentos de Fatima,* pp. 344-352).

God Is Pleased With Your Sacrifices

The September apparition provides us with another very important element in the spiritual life: discretion.

There is a Latin maxim which says, *"In medio stat virtus,"* meaning, "Virtue lies in the middle, in the happy medium."

Jesus Christ and Mary most Holy were the two most balanced persons in the universe.

We, men and women, are always subject to error, permitting ourselves to wander from the straight path. This is why the masters of the spiritual life insist on the need of having recourse regularly to a director who is experienced in the ways of the spirit. They themselves bow to this golden rule. Eminent men like Father De Guibert and Father Vermeersch, of recognized international renown because of their books, wisdom and prudence in the direction of souls, submit themselves humbly, in their turn, to the counsels of their own spiritual directors. This is because nobody is a good judge or physician in his own case.

These considerations are much to the purpose when considering what happened to the three little shepherds. Profoundly impressed by the mystic grace of the vision of Hell, they flung themselves, tooth and nail, into the practice of mortification, going beyond the limits of prudence. This is what Sister Lucia relates:

"Some days later, as we were walking along the road with our sheep, I found a piece of rope that had fallen off a cart. I picked it up, and, just for fun, I tied it round my arm. Before long, I noticed that the rope was hurting me. 'Look, this hurts!' I said to my cousins. 'We could tie it round our waists and offer this sacrifice to God.' The poor children fell in with my suggestion. We then set about dividing it among the three of us, by placing it across a stone and striking it with the sharp edge of another one that served as a knife. Either because of the thickness or roughness of the rope, or because we sometimes tied it too tightly, this instrument of penance often caused us terrible suffering. Now and then, Jacinta could not keep back her tears, so great was the discomfort this caused her. Whenever I urged her to remove it, she replied, 'No! I want to offer this sacrifice to Our Lord in reparation, and for the conversion of sinners.'

"Another day we were playing, picking little plants off the walls and pressing them in our hands to hear them crack. While Jacinta was plucking these plants, she happened to catch hold of some nettles and stung herself. She no sooner felt the pain than she squeezed them more tightly in her hands, and said to us, 'Look! Look! Here is something else with which we can mortify ourselves!' From that time on, we used to hit our legs occasionally with nettles, so as to offer God yet another sacrifice." (*Documentos de Fatima,* pp. 150-152).

Now, according to what the seer relates in reporting the September apparition, the little ones did not undo the rope even at night. So Our Lady had to intervene and admonish them, "God does not wish you to sleep with the rope on." Note, however, that the Most Holy Virgin corrected the exaggerations only, but in no way condemned the practice of mortification. She even assured these innocent children that God was pleased with the sacrifices which they were making, and told them to wear the rope during the day.

Even today some people are indignant about this passage from Sister Lucia's Memoirs, taxing her as unenlightened and the like. In their opinion, voluntary mortification is an intolerable thing in this twentieth century.

The error is not new. Three hundred years ago, Miguel de Molinos declared: "The voluntary cross of mortification is a heavy and fruitless burden, and should therefore be abandoned." Blessed Innocent XI, who ruled the See of Peter at the time, condemned this and many other propositions of the above-mentioned author. (cf. *Dz*. 1258). Nor could it be otherwise, because voluntary mortifications are part of Christian asceticism, with profound roots in the Bible. I have already cited various texts which speak of fasting as a form of penance pleasing to God, and which Jesus Christ Himself embraced. But there are also many passages in Sacred Scripture which speak of hairshirts, coarse garments and other forms of voluntary penance: "Alas for you, Chorazin! Alas for you, Bethsaida! For if the miracles done in you had been done in Tyre and Sidon, they would have repented long ago, sitting in sackcloth and ashes." (*Lk*. 10:13).

"Jacob, tearing his clothes and putting on a loincloth of sackcloth, mourned his son for a long time." (*Gen*. 37:34). "Ahab tore his garments and put sackcloth next to his skin and fasted; he slept in the sackcloth; he walked with slow steps." (*1 K*. 21:27). "David pleaded with Yahweh for the child; he kept a strict fast and went home and spent the night on the bare ground, covered with sacking." (*2 K*. 12:16).

If from these sacred texts, and many others which could be brought forward, we pass on to hagiography, we will see that there is no saint who did not practise, to a greater or lesser degree, voluntary mortification. The reason is given in the *Imitation of Christ:* "In the cross is the height of virtue; in the cross is the perfection of sanctity." (Bk. 2, ch. 12, 2).

There have been saints who were renowned for their

austere penances—some, in overcoming their bad inclinations; others, moved by the ardent desire of resembling, as far as possible, the divine Victim of Golgotha.

This was, for example, the spirituality of the Venerable Maria of the Angels Cruz Guerrero González, foundress of the Company of the Cross, who, at the end of the last century and at the dawn of this, revolutionized the south of Spain with her prodigies of charity, assisting the plague-stricken and all kinds of abandoned people. Only the mystical call of the cross could draw those humble religious to such acts of heroism.

The following passage will give us an idea of the temper of these souls:

"A married couple live in the hive of dwellings at Lampiões. Mother Maria makes a list of the work and assistance recommended to their care for the week. Lampiões, in the district of Macarena and suburbs of Seville, is a collection of squalid homesteads with wretched inhabitants. The two sick people are entirely abandoned. Nobody goes near their door. 'Consumed by smallpox,' as the neighbours say, they do not want to be taken to the public hospital, and of course nobody around will enter their home; on the contrary, when they need to pass their door they go another way round.

'Let's see now, which two sisters will volunteer to look after them.' In such cases, as usual, all raise their hands and then begins the contest as to who will receive the treasure. Mother chooses Sister Milagros.

"On arriving at the place, the sisters sense at once the hostile atmosphere that surrounds the house, and they discover the loathsome room. But Sister Milagros is trained.

"The sisters open a parcel of washed clothing, take off their cloaks and set to work at clothing the sick, dressing their wounds and arranging the bed. The poor sick ones, astounded, cannot believe what they are seeing. The sisters gather the heap of soiled clothing to be washed in the tub, but the housekeeper prevents them. By evening, they return with a large basin and wash the clothing in the middle of

the yard. At night the room shines like a hospital ward. The
sisters don their cloaks and leave the house to return home.
The men of the place are coming from work. One of them
advances on the sisters, uttering blasphemies and shouting
at the housekeeper who has let them in. But she tells all that
has happened, and the entire neighbourhood takes sides
with the sisters. The man speaks to them and asks, 'But they
say there is no God, so why are you doing this?'

"Sister Milagros, who knows where she stands, replies
courageously, 'Yes, brother, yes, God exists and you have
offended Him by blaspheming. For love of Him we would
take care of you too. But you have sinned, and now you
must cry out with me: Long live Christ the King!'

"A week later, the parish priest did not react favourably
when Sister Milagros went with her companion to ask him
to confess the sick in the Lampiões slum.

'To the Lampiões place? Do you know what it is? It's
like an antechamber of Hell. The least we could expect is
not to be let in at all.'

"The priest went, and found a little altar erected in the
centre of the yard, with the housekeeper directing the last
preparations.

"Within ten days there were baptisms, confessions, Mass
and First Communion. The old smallpox patients, com-
forted by the sacraments, passed to another life. The love of
God, and of neighbour for God's sake, so beautifully dem-
onstrated by the sisters, fulfilled in that house an authentic
and holy mission.

"These are the women whom Sister Angela brought into
being." (J. M. Javierre, *Sister Angela of the Cross, Writings
and Intimacies,* Madrid 1974, pp. 124-125).

To love the cross of Christ passionately is an indispensable requisite in order to be able to sacrifice oneself for one's
brothers even to heroism. It is history which says so.

If we look back 340 years, we will encounter St. John of
Brébeuf and his companions: martyrs, stars in the first
ranks of greatness in love of God and neighbour, in the as-

toundingly inhospitable lands of the Hurons.

We would never end if we attempted to catalogue the most austere penances of the Saints which have borne fruit in heroic and disinterested acts in favour of those in need.

But if not all of us are called to imitate this heroism of voluntary austerities, we are at least obliged to respect and admire the power of divine grace in the lives of the saintly souls of all ages, including children like Jacinta and Francisco. It is the Holy Spirit that moves hearts. How uncalled for, then, are those voices raised from time to time against the acts of penance, for example, of those pilgrims who walk all the way to Fatima, and promise to go round the Chapel of the Apparitions on their knees. The faith of these people is worthy of respect.

Necessary Mortification

We are all called to practise the mortification necessary to overcome our evil inclinations. The biblical texts speak of putting these tendencies to death: "If you do live in that way, you are doomed to die; but if by the Spirit you put an end to the misdeeds of the body, you will live." (*Rom.* 8:13).

By misdeeds of the body St. Paul means: "fornication, gross indecency and sexual irresponsibility; idolatry and sorcery; feuds and wrangling, jealousy, bad temper and quarrels; disagreements, factions, envy; murders, drunkenness, orgies and similar things." (*Gal.* 5:19-21).

In another passage he advises, "That is why you must kill everything in you that belongs only to earthly life: fornication, impurity, guilty passion, evil desires and especially greed." (*Col.* 3:5).

All this ascetical struggle has for its aim the resembling of Christ: "Always, wherever we may be, we carry with us in our body the death of Jesus, so that the life of Jesus, too, may always be seen in our body. Indeed, while we are still alive, we are consigned to our death every day, for the sake of Jesus, so that in our mortal flesh the life of Jesus, too, may be openly shown." (*2 Cor.* 4:10-11).

This was the idea which was dominant in the preaching of the Apostle and which emerges spontaneously all through his letters: "You cannot belong to Christ Jesus unless you crucify all self-indulgent passions and desires." (*Gal.* 5:24).

According to the thought of Christ, to embrace the cross is an indispensable condition for following Him, or as one might say, to be saved: "Anyone who does not take his cross and follow in my footsteps is not worthy of me." (*Mt.* 10:38). And Christ's steps are directed on the straight road to Calvary. To him who sought to dissuade Him, He answered in strong terms that were not to be forgotten. "From that time Jesus began to make it clear to his disciples that he was destined to go to Jerusalem and suffer grievously at the hands of the elders and chief priests and scribes, to be put to death and to be raised up on the third day. Then, taking him aside, Peter started to remonstrate with him. 'Heaven preserve you, Lord,' he said, 'this must not happen to you.' But he turned and said to Peter, 'Get behind me, Satan! You are an obstacle in my path, because the way you think is not God's way but man's.'" (*Mt.* 16:21-23).

Let us seek, then, to attune our thoughts and our life to the thoughts of God and the life of Christ.

This is only possible on the strength of much prayer. To this end, St. Paul urged the Christians of Rome, "Work for the Lord with untiring effort and with great earnestness of spirit. If you have hope, this will make you cheerful. Do not give up if trials come; and keep on praying." (*Rom.* 12:11). Indeed, only through perseverance in prayer were these Christians able to attain the ideal which the Apostle proposed to them: "Think of God's mercy, my brothers, and worship him, I beg you, in a way that is worthy of thinking beings, by offering your living bodies as a holy sacrifice, truly pleasing to God. Do not model yourselves on the behaviour of the world around you, but let your behaviour change, modelled by your new mind. This is the only way to discover the will of God and know what is good, what it is that God wants, what is the perfect thing to do." (*Rom.* 12:1-2).

These were not counsels for souls enclosed in convents, but for Christians coming from pagan Rome.

Pray the Rosary

In the previous pages, I have been interlacing commentaries with the recommendations of the Mother of God. It seems to me very advantageous, meanwhile—although it may mean repeating some ideas already exposed—to call attention to yet another point which is mentioned in the six apparitions of the Cova da Iria and in that of Pontevedra. I refer to the prayer of the Rosary.

Let us begin with the texts of Sister Lucia's Memoirs referring to each month:

May: "Pray the Rosary every day, in order to obtain peace for the world, and the end of the war." (*Documentos de Fatima*, p. 332).

June: "I wish you ... to pray the Rosary every day." (*Documentos*, p. 334).

July: "I want you ... to continue to pray the Rosary every day in honour of Our Lady of the Rosary, in order to obtain peace for the world and the end of the war, because only she can help you." (*Documentos*, p.p. 336-338).

August: "I want you ... to continue praying the Rosary every day." (*Documentos*, p. 342).

September: "Continue to pray the Rosary in order to obtain the end of the war." (*Documentos*, p. 346).

October: "I am the Lady of the Rosary. Continue al-
            ways to pray the Rosary every day." (*Docu-
            mentos,* p. 348).

In the apparition of 10 December 1925 in Pontevedra,
Our Lady not only recommended the Rosary, but asked
besides that meditation be made on the mysteries of the
Rosary. (*Documentos,* p. 400).*

In the notes taken by the parish priest of Fatima there are
also references to the Rosary:

July: "I want to tell you . . . to pray the Rosary to
            Our Lady of the Rosary to lessen the war, for
            only she can help you." (*Documentos,* p. 500).

September: "I want to tell you to continue praying the
            Rosary always to Our Lady of the Rosary,
            that she may lessen the war." (*Documentos,* p.
            501).

October: "I want to tell you . . . to pray the Rosary to
            Our Lady. Build a chapel here to Our Lady
            of the Rosary." (*Documentos,* p. 501).

In the various interrogations of the three little shepherds,
carried out by Dr. Formigâo from 27 September 1917 to 2
November of the same year, there also appear references to
the Rosary. Thus, from the questions put to Francisco, it is
known that Our Lady "carries between the palms and the
back of the right hand some beads which hang down over
the dress." Jacinta replies thus to Dr. Formigâo's question:

"What was it that Our Lady recommended most earnestly
to Lucia?"

"She said that we were to pray the Rosary every day."
(*Documentos,* p. 503).

And from the dialogue he had with Lucia on 27 September 1917, he recalls his question:

"Did she tell you and your cousins to say certain
prayers?"

"She told us to say the Rosary in honour of Our Lady of

*The content of this apparition will be developed in the third title in this
series, *Fatima and the Heart of Mary.*

the Rosary, to obtain the peace of the world." (*Documentos,* p. 504).

From this same interview we learn that part of the money left by the people at the foot of the holm oak ought to be used for the cult and the feast of Our Lady of the Rosary.

And from the interrogation of 13 October we learn:

"Did the Lady tell you who she was?"

"She said that she was the Lady of the Rosary."

"Did you ask her what she wanted?"

"Yes."

"What did she say?"

"She said that we were to amend our lives and not offend Our Lord any more because He was too much offended already, and that we were to say the Rosary and ask pardon for our sins." (*Documentos,* p. 508).

After such expressive passages, it was not surprising to hear the Holy Father declare in the Chapel of the Apparitions: "I have come on pilgrimage to Fatima . . . with the Rosary in my hand. Fatima speaks to us so much of the Rosary—of the recitation of the third part of the Rosary—as the little shepherds said. The Rosary, its third part, is and always will remain a prayer of gratitude, of love and faithful entreaty—the prayer of the Mother of the Church! . . . Pray very much, pray the Rosary every day."

It is not only John Paul II who prays the Rosary daily and counsels all the members of the Church to do the same. His predecessors in the chair of Peter have never tired of insisting on this devotion so dear to the Mother of God. Hundreds of pages would scarcely suffice to contain excerpts from pontifical documents relating to the Rosary.* The reason for this attitude is very simple: The Rosary, when prayed properly, leads us to meditation on the principal mysteries of the life of the Son of God—the Incarna-

---

*Pope Leo XIII alone published eleven such encyclical letters: *Supremi apostolatus, Superiore anno, Quamque pluries, Octobri mense, Magnae Dei Matris, Laetitiae sanctae, Jucundae semper, Adjutricem populi, Fidentem piumque, Augustissima Virginis, Diuturni temporis.*

tion, Death and Resurrection of our Saviour. It leads us to
intimacy with the Most Holy Trinity.

Many people lack devotion to the Rosary because they
have never tried to pray it as it should be prayed. They
begin to imagine Our Lady away up in Heaven, as if she
were a million miles distant. No one can pray the Rosary, or
any other prayer, in this way. When we are about to pray,
we must understand that the Kingdom of God is within us
(cf. *Lk.* 17:21), that Christ is in the Father, and we in
Christ and Christ in us. (cf. *Jn.* 14:20). When we decide to
pray the Rosary, therefore, we need to arouse our faith in
the fact that we are going *to speak to Our Lady who is present with us, who listens to us and who loves us.* We begin by
addressing her with the well-known salutation of the angel:
Hail, full of grace. We rejoice with her and congratulate
her because Almighty God, Lord of the Universe, the only
One who can make people truly happy, loves her infinitely:
the Lord is with you. And for this reason, she is blessed
among women. But not only is she happy by feeling within
herself, in a living way, the friendship of God; He it is who
is to be born of her as well: **and blessed is the fruit of your
womb, Jesus.**

After congratulating the Blessed Virgin Mary on the titles
and privileges which to her are most dear and honourable,
let us begin to make our petitions.

And what are we going to ask?

For everything we wish, and which we need now at this
moment of our life.

Is there something which worries us, which is a source of
anguish to us?

Let us turn confidently to Mary, to the Mother of Him
who is Omnipotent, who has recommended to us and
guaranteed: *Ask, and you shall receive.*

Therefore, we pray: "Holy Mary, Mother of God, pray
for us sinners, now and at the hour of our death. Amen."

In this **pray for us** are included all the men, women and
children of the world:

The dying, who at every moment are passing into eternity; those who are suffering, either because they have nothing to eat, or because they are victims of injustice, hate, senseless wars, earthquakes, bad weather or illness; the orphans, the widows, the innocent in prison; those who have lost their faith; those who have set out on a path of vice and crime; those who die daily on the roads; the parents who grieve so much for their children; the children and youth, that they may not be disappointed in their hopes; priests and religious, that they may remain faithful to their vocation.

"The Rosary prayer embraces the problems of the Church, of the See of Peter, the problems of the whole world," Pope John Paul II declared in his homily at Fatima. "In it we also remember sinners, that they may be converted and saved, and the souls in Purgatory."

"Pray for us sinners, now and at the **hour of our death.**" Yes, we pray for what we need at this present moment of our existence, but we pray, above all, that the Mother of God may assist us in that decisive hour of our departure into eternity.

Now if we pray daily for this grace, there is no reason for us to fear death, because at that hour we will undoubtedly have at our side, smiling, the Mother of Him who is going to judge us, and who is also our Mother.

But the prayer of the Rosary contains yet other attractions. Between each decade, we address the Most Holy Trinity in a hymn of praise: **Glory be to the Father, and to the Son, and to the Holy Spirit.** It is the opportune moment to recall that we are the living temples of that same august Trinity: "If anyone loves me he will keep my word, and my Father will love him, and we shall come to him and make our home with him." (*Jn.* 14:23). "I shall ask the Father and he will give you another Advocate to be with you for ever, the Spirit of truth . . . who is in you." (*Jn.* 14:16-17). "Your body, you know, is the temple of the Holy Spirit, who is in you." (*1 Cor.* 6:19).

Besides the **Glory be,** we pray the prayer which Jesus taught to the Apostles: the **Our Father.**

These words ought to awaken within us sentiments of good will to live as worthy children of such a Father. In considering this reality, St. John was deeply stirred: "Think of the love that the Father has lavished on us, by letting us be called God's children; and that is what we are." (*1 Jn.* 3:1). And with logical accuracy, he drew the conclusions from such a marvel: "My dear people, since God has loved us so much, we too should love one another." (*1 Jn.* 4:11). Well, the first consequence of love is the pardoning of offenses, of quarrels, of misunderstandings. Therefore, Christ, in the Our Father, taught us to pray: **Forgive us our trespasses as we forgive those who trespass against us.**

From all these considerations, one can see how the praying of the Rosary in the family would be the most efficacious means to calm the small and great storms that perchance may arise between husband and wife, parents and children, brothers among themselves. St. Paul's recommendation is worthy of meditation: "Even if you are angry, you must not sin: never let the sun set on your anger, or else you will give the devil a foothold . . . Never have grudges against others, or lose your temper, or blaspheme, or raise your voice to anybody, or call each other names, or allow any sort of spitefulness. Be merciful with one another, and kind, forgiving each other as readily as God forgave you in Christ." (*Eph.* 4:26-27, 31-32).

Some there are who do not pray the Rosary, it being too monotonous to repeat the *Ave Maria* fifty times. But it happens that such persons may allow themselves to be carried away by modern songs which are limited to strident sounds centred on one phrase that is often meaningless and even in bad taste.

The Rosary never becomes monotonous for those who love the Mother of God and of the Church. On the contrary, the more it is prayed and meditated, the more unction they draw from it.

The holy, friendly and good Pope John XXIII confided these words to his diary during a retreat he made in the Vatican from November 26 to December 2, 1961: "It gives me joy to keep faithful to my religious practises: Holy Mass, the Divine Office, the whole Rosary, with meditation on the mysteries, constant preoccupation with God and with spiritual things." (*Journal of a Soul,* p. 319).

A scene that was very revealing of his character, so simple and averse to formalism, took place during the visit of Agiubei, director of the Soviet newspaper *Izvestia*, with his wife Rada Khrushcheva, Khrushchev's daughter:

"At one stage, the Pope took a rosary from the table and spoke to Rada: 'My dear lady, this is for you. You know, I was told that to a non-Catholic princess I should present coins or stamps or books . . . But I am giving you a rosary just the same. We priests have, besides the biblical prayer of the Psalms which is the Breviary, these fifteen Mysteries which are fifteen windows from which I see, in the light of God, all that is happening in the world. And I pray and pray. I say one Rosary in the morning, another in the afternoon and another at night. Look, the journalists were very impressed when I told them this morning that I prayed for them in the fifth Joyful Mystery. When, on the other hand, I pray the third Joyful Mystery and meditate on the birth of Jesus, I remember all the children who have come into the world during the last twenty-four hours, so that, whether Catholics or not, they have the prayers and wishes of the Pope to start off in life. When I pray the third Joyful Mystery, I will remember your children also, my dear lady."
(*Joao XXIII,* Edicoes Salesianas, Porto 1968, pp. 188-189).

The Popes not only pray the Rosary, the complete daily Rosary, and recommend it as a customary form of prayer in the home, but they have also enriched it with a plenary indulgence, when prayed in church, public oratory, in the family, community or pious association.

The day has 1,440 minutes. If we take fifteen or twenty minutes for the praying of the Rosary, we still have 1,420 left for work, rest and other occupations.

But the most convincing argument which should impel us to embrace this devotion is that *it was this prayer and no other* which Our Lady proclaimed to be most pleasing to her.

There are people who, when they want a favour of someone, usually offer a present in order to win over the person who is in a position to grant what they desire. Obviously they seek to offer a gift that will please the person on whom the favour depends. Of course, it is not always easy to discover the preferences of this particular person. However, in the case of the Blessed Virgin Mary, that difficulty does not exist, because *she herself has deigned to let us know what pleases her most,* through the intermediary of three innocent children and, above all, through the voice and example of the Roman Pontiffs, Representatives and Vicars of her divine Son.

Only She Can Help You

We have seen that in the notes made by the parish priest of Fatima, he recorded this phrase spoken by the Apparition: "I want to tell you . . . to pray the Rosary to Our Lady of the Rosary to lessen the war, for only she can help you."

However strange that it may seem, this is another phrase of great theological depth!

Let us return to Sacred Scripture.

In the desert, the people of God sinned gravely against the Lord who had mercifully liberated them from the slavery of Egypt. God communicated to Moses His intention of destroying this stiff-necked people. Moses implored mercy and Israel, figure of the Church, was saved.

How much more precious than the prayer of Moses is the intercession of the Blessed Virgin Mary, Mother of God!

This limitless power was bestowed on her by the eternal

Father, in choosing her to be Mother of the Word Incarnate: "When the appointed time came, God sent his Son, born of a woman." (*Gal.* 4:4).

The appointed time!

The beginning had been billions of years before: "In the beginning God created the heavens and the earth." (*Gen.* 1:1). Before that there had been no time! Only eternity! St. John penetrated into this Sanctuary: "In the beginning was the Word: the Word was with God and the Word was God. He was with God in the beginning. Through him all things came to be, not one thing had its being but through him." (*Jn.* 1:1-3).

In the beginning God created the heavens and the earth!

"Let us contemplate the celestial firmament on a clear and moonless night. Those innumerable luminous dots which sprinkle it are no more than specks in the vast assembly that is the Galaxy or Milky Way, but which is actually only one among millions and millions of other similar assemblies of stars, designated as galaxies . . .

"The Milky Way, with a total mass that should be equivalent to 200 thousand million times our sun, constitutes an impressive assembly of stars (more than 100 thousand million units) of gaseous matter." (Verbo *Universal Atlas,* p. 38).

Those who have studied this science speak of swarms or clusters of galaxies and say that "they are generally known by the names of the constellations in which they appear; an example is that of Virgo.

"The Virgo group is the nearest and the most conspicuous of the greater clusters, situated at a distance initially calculated at 20 million light-years." (R.H. Baker, *Astronomia,* Lisbon 1971, p. 566).

Knowing that the speed of light is 300,000 kilometers per second, our imagination is lost in the effort of contemplating a distance such as "20 million light-years."

Such is the power of God! In the beginning He created the heavens and the earth.

But if the unimaginable greatness of the material universe causes us astonishment, what can we say then of that which St. Paul refers to in these verses: "When the appointed time came, God sent His Son, born of a woman."

Jesus Christ and Mary Most Holy are, as it were, the apex of the power and the wisdom of God!

Jesus Christ is Man and God! He is a most perfect Man, with a body and soul like ours. But this human nature is hypostatically united to the Divine Nature in the Person of the Eternal Word. Jesus, therefore, responds emphatically to the Jews who attack Him: "I tell you most solemnly, before Abraham ever was, I Am." (*Jn.* 8:58). At that moment, His hearers must have recalled the passage from Exodus: "Then Moses said to God, 'I am to go, then, to the sons of Israel and say to them, "The God of your fathers has sent me to you." But if they ask me what his name is, what am I to tell them?' And God said to Moses, 'I Am who I Am. This,' he added, 'is what you must say to the sons of Israel: "I Am has sent me to you."'" (*Ex.* 3:13-14).

And because Jesus Christ is the eternal "I Am," He could come to earth and remain in Heaven: "No one has gone up to heaven except the one who came down from heaven, the Son of Man who is in heaven." (*Jn.* 3: 13). It is because He is One (one nature) with the Father: "Have I been with you all this time, Philip, and you still do not know me? To have seen me is to have seen the Father, so how can you say, 'Let us see the Father'? Do you not believe that I am in the Father and the Father is in me?" (*Jn.* 14:9-10). Or more explicitly: "The Father and I are one." (*Jn.* 10:30).

Jesus Christ is true Man and true God! As a man, He was born, lived and died. As God, He rose by His own power: "Destroy this sanctuary, and in three days I will raise it up." (*Jn.* 2:19).

St. John explains that "He was speaking of the sanctuary that was his body, and when Jesus rose from the dead, his disciples remembered that he had said this, and they

believed the scripture and the words he had said." (*Jn.* 2:
21-22).

The most explicit profession of faith was that of Thomas:
"My Lord and my God!" (*Jn.* 20:28).

Throughout the entire Gospel of St. John, the Divinity of
Christ is placed in high relief: "No one has ever seen God;
it is the only Son, who is nearest to the Father's heart, who
has made him known." (*Jn.* 1:18).

Mary Mediatrix

The wonder of wonders is that "the only Son, who is
nearest to the Father's heart," "when the appointed time
came," entered the world through a woman, who was a
virgin and remained a virgin, who was immaculate and was
preserved immaculate forever.

Oh, prodigy of prodigies: Mary most Holy is a creature,
and Mother of the Creator!

To recount here the glories and privileges of this woman,
would be for me an immeasurable joy, but it would exceed
the limits of this work.

Nevertheless, so that the meaning of this phrase may be
understood—"only she can help you"—I cannot omit to
give prominence to the role that Mary fulfilled and continues to fulfill in the history of the New Covenant or in the
Mystery of the Church:

—She gave her consent to the Incarnation of the Word.
(cf. *Lk.* 1:38).

—With her presence, the precursor of the Messiah (cf.
Lk. 1:44), link in the union between the Old and New
Covenant, was sanctified in his mother's womb.

—She it was who gave birth to the Son of the Most High.
(cf. *Lk.* 1:31-32).

—She it was who showed the Child Jesus to the
shepherds, the first heralds of the Good News (cf. *Lk.*

2:16-17), and to the Wise Men who came from the East (cf. *Mt.* 2:11), figure of all the peoples who were to believe in Christ.

—She carried Him to the Temple, to present Him to the Lord. There, Simeon recognized in that Child the "Light to enlighten the nations" and prophesied that this would only come about through the sufferings of the Mother: "A sword will pierce your own soul too." (*Lk.* 2:35).

—She defended the life of the Son of God from the murderous wrath of Herod, flying into Egypt with her most chaste spouse. (cf. *Mt.* 2:13-15).

—Through her prayers in Cana of Galilee, Jesus, anticipating the hour when He was to reveal His power to work miracles, worked the first miracle, and "his disciples believed in him." (*Jn.* 2:11). The Most Blessed Virgin thus began to fulfill her function of Mediatrix, which should be understood in the sense given to it by Vatican Council II:

"This motherhood of Mary in the order of grace continues uninterruptedly from the consent which she loyally gave at the Annunciation and which she sustained without wavering beneath the cross, until the eternal fulfillment of all the elect. Taken up to Heaven, she did not lay aside this saving office, but by her manifold intercession continues to bring us the gifts of eternal salvation. By her maternal charity, she cares for the brethren of her Son, who still journey on earth surrounded by dangers and difficulties, until they are led into their blessed home. Therefore, the Blessed Virgin is invoked in the Church under the titles of Advocate, Helper, Benefactress, and Mediatrix. This, however, is so understood that it neither takes away anything from, nor adds anything to the dignity and efficacy of Christ the one Mediator.

"No creature could ever be counted along with the Incarnate Word and Redeemer; but just as the priesthood of Christ is shared in various ways both by His ministers and the faithful, and as the one goodness of God is radiated in different ways among His creatures, so also the unique mediation of the Redeemer does not exclude, but rather gives rise to a manifold cooperation which is but a sharing in this one source.

"The Church does not hesitate to profess this subordinate role of Mary, which it constantly experiences and recommends to the heartfelt attention of the faithful, so that encouraged by this maternal help they may the more closely adhere to the Mediator and Redeemer." (*Lumen Gentium,* 62).

If "the motherhood of Mary continues uninterruptedly," if "by her manifold intercession she continues to bring us the gifts of eternal salvation, and cares for the brethren of her Son, who still journey on earth surrounded by dangers and difficulties"—how is it that there are doubts as to the meaning of the phrase: "Only she can help you"?

Of course, it is obvious that Mary is not trying to put herself in God's place, but only to admonish some of her misguided children who would attempt to lower her from the place bestowed on her by God in the history of salvation, and furthermore, to warn all peoples that peace is not obtained exclusively by human means.

Mary Is the Most Direct Way to Christ

Thanks be to God that there are lessening numbers of those who attack the devotion to Our Lady openly, on the false pretext of giving Christ the place that is due to Him.

Already in 1976, in the prologue of the book, *Documentos,* I wrote: "These supposed defenders of the Son of God forget that there is no Saint or Blessed who has not been very devoted to the Virgin Mary. And this devotion does not impede their being united intimately to Christ and dedicated heroically in the service of their brothers. In their turn, the seers of Fatima developed a spiritual life that is a categorical and formal confirmation of the same. In fact, on first sight, we might be led to imagine that the spirit of the three children had been so intensely fascinated by the Blessed Virgin that it would have been difficult, if not impossible, for them to think of Christ. And what do Sister Lucia's writings reveal? Exactly the contrary: Francisco, for example, despite the words of the Apparition, 'He must say many Rosaries' (p. 331), frequently exclaimed, 'I love God so much! But He is very sad because of so many sins!' (pp. 259-285), and, 'If only I could give Him joy!' (p. 261). 'Listen! You go to school, and I'll stay here in the church, close to the hidden Jesus.' (p. 287).

"The conclusion is evident: Devotion to the Mother of God does not impede souls in their rapid ascension to Christ, but rather favours it and gives it impetus." (*Documentos de Fatima*, xiii).

But it is not enough to refrain from attacking devotion to Our Lady theoretically. We must needs put an end to the attitude of segregating her from our day-to-day spiritual life. There are seminaries and religious houses where prayer is limited to Mass and to part of the Liturgy of the Hours. There is no place for Mary in the spiritual life of these souls. They are orphaned from their Mother!

If the Eternal Father united Jesus and Mary so intimately—when the appointed time came, God sent His Son, born of a woman—how can one attain intimate union with Christ, while putting aside devotion to the Mother of the Word Incarnate?

Do not they who act like this notice that Mary, the loving and attentive Mother, accompanied the Apostles, the pillars of the Church, praying with them at the dawning of the same Church? And that all the Apostles were praying with Mary? (cf. *Acts* 1:12-14).

Great hearts are those which have the capacity to love Christ and all the saints, to love Christ and all men.

On the contrary, exclusivism is proper to niggardly

hearts. John Paul II has a great heart, an immense heart. He loves Christ passionately. But this does not prevent him from professing his esteem for Mary: TOTUS TUUS!

"The words *'Totus Tuus'* ('All Yours') are related wholly to Mary. 'All Yours' in total consecration to Mary, in complete and filial devotion to the Virgin Mary! They are the motto of his life, of his heart, of his pastoral action. He has thus expressed himself: 'I wish to be united to Christ in the priesthood and in pastoral service through Mary, His Mother. Her place in the history of salvation is little known. We wish to enter into it ever more deeply and place it in relief, for Mary fulfills a role that is totally unique in the redemption brought about by Christ. For a long time now I have been convinced that without her it is extremely difficult to enter into Christ's life-work.'" (F. Leite, *John Paul II,* Braga 1982, p. 97).

This passionate love for Christ and Mary has led the Pope to be truly a man of prayer. According to those close to him, "he devotes about five hours daily to prayer." (*op. cit,* p. 88).

Vatican Council II is no less expressive regarding the Mother of God:

"The sacred synod teaches this Catholic doctrine advisedly and at the same time admonishes all the sons of the Church that the cult, especially the liturgical cult, of the Blessed Virgin, be generously fostered, and that the practices and exercises of devotion towards her, recommended by the teaching authority of the Church in the course of centuries, be highly esteemed, and that those decrees which were given in the early days regarding the cult of images of Christ, the Blessed Virgin and the saints, be religiously observed." (*Lumen Gentium,* 67).

To cherish a high esteem for the Rosary is indeed recommended by the Council, although expressed in other words. Besides, the Fathers of Vatican II also declare:

"Wishing in His supreme goodness and wisdom to effect the redemption of the world 'when the fullness of time came, God sent his Son, born of a woman . . . that we might receive the adoption of sons.' (*Gal.* 4:4). 'He, for us men, and for our salvation, came down from heaven, and was incarnate by the Holy Spirit from the Virgin Mary.' This divine mystery of salvation is revealed to us and continued in the Church, which the Lord established as His body. Joined to Christ the Head and in communion with all His Saints, the faithful must in the first place reverence the memory 'of the glorious ever Virgin Mary, Mother of God and of Our Lord Jesus Christ.'" (*Lumen Gentium,* 52).

And why is this? The same Council states:

"The Virgin Mary . . . the beloved daughter of the Father and the temple of the Holy Spirit . . . far surpasses all creatures, both in Heaven and on earth. But, being of the race of Adam, she is at the same time also united to all those who are to be saved; indeed, 'she is clearly the Mother of the members of Christ . . . since she has by her charity joined in bringing about the birth of believers in the Church, who are members of its Head.' Wherefore she is hailed as pre-eminent and as a wholly unique member of the Church, and as its type and outstanding model in faith and charity. The Catholic Church, taught by the Holy Spirit, honors charity. The Catholic Church, taught by the Holy Spirit, honors her with filial affection and devotion as a most beloved Mother." (*Lumen Gentium,* 53).

From these documents and others which could be cited, we conclude:

1. Whoever in his spiritual life does not cultivate a filial piety towards the Mother of God and of the Church, is not attuned to the teachings of Vatican Council II.

2. Whoever fails to pray the Rosary daily deviates from the example given by the Popes, and disobeys their constant recommendations. In Fatima alone, John Paul II mentioned the word "Rosary" or its third part eleven times, and recommended: "Pray much; pray the Rosary every day."

3. The Message of Fatima—which places special emphasis on the responsibility laid on all the baptized, members of the Mystical Body, for the salvation of all, by means of prayer and sacrifice united to the sufferings of Christ—is profoundly evangelical. In fact, this was exactly what John Paul II stressed with redoubled vigour: "The appeal of the Lady of the Message of Fatima is so deeply rooted in the Gospel and the whole of Tradition that *the Church feels that the message imposes a commitment on her.*"

So that readers may the more easily appreciate and meditate the words of the homily delivered by the Holy Father at the solemn Mass celebrated on 13 May 1982, in the Cova da Iria, the complete text is given here. It is the golden key that closes these pages.

III

HOMILY OF POPE JOHN PAUL II
at Fatima on 13 May 1982

1. "And from that hour the disciple took her to his own home." (*Jn.* 19:27).

These are the concluding words of the Gospel in today's liturgy at Fatima. The disciple's name was John. It was he, John the son of Zebedee, the Apostle and Evangelist, who heard from the cross the words of Christ: "Behold your mother." But first Christ had said to His Mother, "Woman, behold your son." This was a wonderful testament.

As He left this world, Christ gave to His Mother a man, a human being, to be like a son for her: John. He entrusted him to her. And, as a consequence of this giving and entrusting, Mary became the mother of John. The Mother of God became the Mother of man.

From that hour, John "took her to his own home" and became the earthly guardian of the Mother of his Master; for sons have the right and duty to care for their mother. John became by Christ's will the son of the Mother of God. And in John every human being became her child.

The Mother's Presence

2. The words "he took her to his own home" can be taken in the literal sense as referring to the place where he lived. Mary's motherhood in our regard is manifested in a

particular way in the places where she meets us: her dwelling places; places in which a special presence of the Mother is felt.

There are many such dwelling places. They are of all kinds; from a special corner in the home or little wayside shrines adorned with an image of the Mother of God, to chapels and churches built in her honour. However, in certain places the Mother's presence is felt in a particularly vivid way. These places sometimes radiate their light over a great distance and draw people from afar. Their radiance may extend over a diocese, a whole nation, or at times over several countries and even continents. These places are the Marian sanctuaries or shrines.

In all these places that unique testament of the Crucified Lord is wonderfully actualized: in them man feels that he is entrusted and confided to Mary; he goes there in order to be with her, as with his Mother; he opens his heart to her and speaks to her about everything; he "takes her to his own home," that is to say, he brings her into all his problems, which at times are difficult—his own problems and those of others; the problems of the family, of societies, of nations, and of the whole of humanity.

Through God's Mercy

3. Is not this the case with the shrine at Lourdes, in France? Is not this the case with Jasna Gora, in Poland, my own country's shrine, which this year is celebrating its six hundredth anniversary?

There too, as in so many other shrines of Mary throughout the world, the words of today's liturgy seem to resound with a particularly authentic force: "You are the great pride of our nation" (*Judith* 15:9), and also: "When our nation was brought low . . . you avenged our ruin, walking in the straight path before our God." (*Judith* 13:20).

At Fatima these words resound as one particular echo of the experiences not only of the Portuguese nation, but also of so many other countries and peoples on this earth, indeed, they echo the experience of modern mankind as a whole, the whole of the human family.

4. And so I come here today because on this very day last year, in St. Peter's Square in Rome, the attempt on the Pope's life was made, in mysterious coincidence with the anniversary of the first apparition at Fatima, which occurred on 13 May 1917.

I seemed to recognize in the coincidence of the dates a special call to come to this place. And so, today I am here. I have come in order to thank Divine Providence in this place which the Mother of God seems to have chosen in a particular way. *"Misericordiae Domini, quia non sumus consumpti"* ("Through God's mercy we were spared"—*Lam.* 2:22), I repeat once more with the prophet.

I have come especially in order to confess here the glory of God Himself:

"Blessed be the Lord God, who created the heavens and the earth," I say in the words of today's liturgy. (*Judith* 13:18).

And to the Creator of Heaven and earth I also raise that special hymn of glory which is she herself, the Immaculate Mother of the Incarnate Word:

"O daughter, you are blessed by the Most High God above all women on earth . . . your hope will never depart from the hearts of men, as they remember the power of God. May God grant this to be a perpetual honour to you." (*Judith* 13:24).

At the basis of this song of praise, which the Church lifts up with joy here as in so many other places on the earth, is the incomparable choice of a daughter of the human race to be the Mother of God.

And therefore let God above all be praised: Father, Son and Holy Spirit. May blessing and veneration be given to Mary, the model of the Church, as the "dwelling place of the Most Holy Trinity."

Spiritual Motherhood

5. From the time when Jesus, dying on the cross, said to John: "Behold your mother"; from the time when "the disciple took her to his own home," the mystery of the spiritual motherhood of Mary has been actualized boundlessly in history. Motherhood means caring for the life of the child. Since Mary is the Mother of us all, her care for the life of man is universal. The care of a mother embraces her child totally. Mary's motherhood has its beginning in her motherly care for Christ. In Christ, at the foot of the cross, she accepted John, and in John she accepted all of us totally. Mary embraces us all with special solicitude in the Holy Spirit. For as we profess in our Creed, He is "the Giver of life." It is He who gives the fullness of life, open towards eternity.

Mary's spiritual motherhood is therefore a sharing in the power of the Holy Spirit, of "the Giver of life." It is the humble service of her who says of herself: "Behold, I am the handmaid of the Lord." (*Lk.* 1:38).

In the light of the mystery of Mary's spiritual motherhood, let us seek to understand the extraordinary message, which began on 13 May 1917 to resound throughout the world from Fatima, continuing for five months until 13 October of the same year.

Convert and Repent

6. The Church has always taught and continues to proclaim that God's revelation was brought to completion in Jesus Christ, who is the Fullness of that revelation, and that "no new public revelation is to be expected before the glorious manifestation of Our Lord." (*Dei Verbum,* 4). The Church evaluates and judges private revelations by the criterion of conformity with that single public Revelation.

If the Church has accepted the Message of Fatima, it is above all because that message contains a truth and a call whose basic content is the truth and the call of the Gospel itself.

"Repent, and believe in the gospel" (*Mk.* 1:15): These are the first words that the Messiah addressed to humanity. The Message of Fatima is, in its basic nucleus, a call to conversion and repentance, as in the Gospel. This call was uttered at the beginning of the twentieth century, and it was thus addressed particularly to this present century. The Lady of the message seems to have read with special insight the "signs of the times," the signs of our time.

The call to repentance is a motherly one, and at the same time it is strong and decisive. The love that "rejoices in the truth" (cf. *1 Cor.* 13) is capable of being clear-cut and firm. The call to repentance is linked, as always, with a call to prayer. In harmony with the tradition of many centuries, the Lady of the message indicates the Rosary, which can rightly be defined as "Mary's prayer," the prayer in which she feels particularly united with us. She herself prays with us. The Rosary prayer embraces the problems of the Church, of the See of Peter, the problems of the whole world. In it we also remember sinners, that they may be converted and saved, and the souls in Purgatory.

The words of the message were addressed to children aged from seven to ten. Children, like Bernadette of Lourdes, are particularly privileged in these apparitions of the Mother of God. Hence the fact that also her language is simple, within the limits of their understanding. The children of Fatima became partners in dialogue with the Lady of the message and collaborators with her. One of them is still living.

The Love of the Saviour's Mother

7. When Jesus on the cross said, "Woman, behold your son" (*Jn.* 19:26), in a new way He opened His Mother's heart, the Immaculate Heart, and revealed to it the new dimensions and extent of the love to which she was called in the Holy Spirit by the power of the sacrifice of the cross.

In the words of Fatima we seem to find this dimension of motherly love, whose range covers the whole of man's path towards God; the path that leads through this world and that goes, through Purgatory, beyond this world. The solicitude of the Mother of the Saviour is solicitude for the work of salvation: the work of her Son. It is solicitude for the salvation, the eternal salvation, of all. Now that sixty-five years have passed since that 13 May 1917, it is difficult to fail to notice how the range of this salvific love of the Mother embraces, in a particular way, our century.

In the light of a mother's love we understand the whole message of the Lady of Fatima. The greatest obstacle to man's journey towards God is sin, perseverance in sin, and finally, denial of God. The deliberate blotting out of God from the world of human thought. The detachment from Him of the whole of man's earthly activity. The rejection of God by man.

In reality, the eternal salvation of man is only in God. Man's rejection of God, if it becomes definitive, leads logically to God's rejection of man (cf. *Mt.* 7:23; 10:33), to damnation.

Can the Mother who, with all the force of the love that she fosters in the Holy Spirit, desires everyone's salvation, keep silence on what undermines the very bases of their salvation? No, she cannot.

And so, while the message of Our Lady of Fatima is a motherly one, it is also strong and decisive. It sounds severe. It sounds like John the Baptist speaking on the banks of the Jordan. It invites to repentance. It gives a warning. It calls to prayer. It recommends the Rosary.

The message is addressed to every human being. The love of the Saviour's Mother reaches every place touched by the work of salvation. Her care extends to every individual of our time, and to all the societies, nations and peoples. Societies menaced by apostasy, threatened by moral degradation. The collapse of morality involves the collapse of societies.

The Meaning of Consecration

8. On the cross Christ said, "Woman, behold your son!" With these words He opened in a new way His Mother's heart. A little later, the Roman soldier's spear pierced the side of the Crucified One. That pierced heart became a sign of the redemption achieved through the death of the Lamb of God.

The Immaculate Heart of Mary, opened with the words, "Woman, behold your son!" is spiritually united with the heart of her Son, opened by the soldier's spear. Mary's heart was opened by the same love for man and for the world with which Christ loved man and the world, offering Himself for them on the cross, until the soldier's spear struck that blow.

Consecrating the world to the Immaculate Heart of Mary means drawing near, through the Mother's intercession, to the very Fountain of life that sprang from Golgotha. This Fountain unceasingly pours forth redemption and grace. In it reparation is made continually for the sins of the world. It is a ceaseless source of new life and holiness.

Consecrating the world to the Immaculate Heart of the Mother means returning beneath the cross of the Son. It means consecrating this world to the pierced heart of the Saviour, bringing it back to the very source of its Redemption. Redemption is always greater than man's sin and the "sin of the world." The power of the Redemption is infinitely superior to the whole range of evil in man and of the world.

The heart of the Mother is aware of this, more than any other heart in the whole universe, visible and invisible.

And so she calls us.

She not only calls us to be converted; she calls us to accept her motherly help to return to the Source of Redemption.

9. Consecrating ourselves to Mary means accepting her help to offer ourselves and the whole of mankind to Him who is holy, infinitely holy; it means accepting her help—by having recourse to her motherly heart, which beneath the cross was opened to love for every human being, for the whole world—in order to offer the world, the individual human being, mankind as a whole, and all the nations to Him who is infinitely holy. God's holiness showed itself in the redemption of man, of the world, of the whole of mankind, and of the nations: a Redemption brought about through the sacrifice of the cross. "For their sake I consecrate myself," Jesus had said. (*Jn.* 17:19).

By the power of the Redemption, the world and man have been consecrated. They have been consecrated to Him who is infinitely holy. They have been offered and entrusted to Love itself, merciful Love.

The Mother of Christ calls us, invites us to join with the Church of the living God in the consecration of the world, in this act of confiding by which the world, mankind as a whole, the nations, each individual person are presented to the Eternal Father with the power of the Redemption won by Christ. They are offered in the heart of the Redeemer which was pierced on the cross.

Rooted in the Gospel

10. The appeal of the Lady of the Message of Fatima is so deeply rooted in the Gospel and the whole of Tradition that the Church feels that the message imposes a commitment on her.

She has responded through the Servant of God Pius XII (whose episcopal ordination took place precisely on 13 May 1917): He consecrated the human race and especially the peoples of Russia to the Immaculate Heart of Mary. Was not that consecration his response to the evangelical eloquence of the call of Fatima?

In its *Dogmatic Constitution on the Church* (*Lumen Gentium*) and its *Pastoral Constitution on the Church in the Modern World* (*Gaudium et Spes*), the Second Vatican Council amply illustrated the reasons for the link between the Church and the world of today. Furthermore, its teaching on Mary's special place in the Mystery of Christ and the Church bore mature fruit in Paul VI's action in calling Mary "Mother of the Church" and thus indicating more profoundly the nature of her union with the Church and of her care for the world, for mankind, for each human being, and for all the nations; what characterizes them is her motherhood.

This brought a further deepening of understanding of the meaning of the act of consecrating that the Church is called upon to perform with the help of the Heart of Christ's Mother and ours.

The Denial of God

11. Today John Paul II, successor of Peter, continuer of the work of Pius, John and Paul, and particular heir of the Second Vatican Council, presents himself before the Mother of the Son of God in her shrine at Fatima. In what way does he come?

He presents himself, reading again with trepidation the motherly call to penance, to conversion, the ardent appeal of the Heart of Mary that resounded at Fatima sixty-five years ago. Yes, he reads it again with trepidation in his heart, because he sees how many people and societies—how many Christians—have gone in the opposite direction to the one indicated in the Message of Fatima. Sin has thus made itself firmly at home in the world, and denial of God has become widespread in the ideologies, ideas and plans of human beings.

But for this very reason the evangelical call to repentance and conversion, uttered in the Mother's message, remains ever relevant. It is still more relevant than it was sixty-five years ago. It is still more urgent. And so it is to be the subject of next year's Synod of Bishops, for which we are already preparing.

The successor of Peter presents himself here also as a witness to the immensity of human suffering, a witness to the almost apocalyptic menaces looming over the nations and mankind as a whole. He is trying to embrace these sufferings with his own weak human heart, as he places himself before the mystery of the heart of the Mother, the Immaculate Heart of Mary.

In the name of these sufferings and with awareness of the evil that is spreading throughout the world and menacing the individual human being, the nations, and mankind as a whole, Peter's successor presents himself here with greater faith in the Redemption of the world, in the saving Love that is always stronger, always more powerful than any evil.

My heart is oppressed when I see the sin of the world and

the whole range of menaces gathering like a dark cloud over mankind, but it also rejoices with hope as I once more do what has been done by my predecessors, when they consecrated the world to the heart of the Mother, when they consecrated especially to that heart those peoples which particularly need to be consecrated. Doing this means consecrating the world to Him who is infinite Holiness. This Holiness means redemption. It means a love more powerful than evil. No "sin of the world" can ever overcome this Love.

Once more this act is being done. Mary's appeal is not for just once. Her appeal must be taken up by generation after generation, in accordance with the ever new "signs of the times." It must be unceasingly returned to. It must ever be taken up anew.

The Faith of the Church

12. The author of the Apocalypse wrote: "And I saw the holy city, new Jerusalem, coming down out of heaven from God, prepared as a bride adorned for her husband; and I heard a loud voice from the throne saying, 'Behold, the dwelling of God is with men. He will dwell with them, and they shall be his people, and God himself will be with them.'" (*Rev.* 21: 2-3).

This is the faith by which the Church lives.

This is the faith with which the People of God makes its journey.

"The dwelling of God is with men" on earth even now.

In that dwelling is the heart of the Bride and Mother, Mary, a heart adorned with the jewel of her Immaculate Conception. The heart of the Bride and Mother which was opened beneath the cross by the word of her Son to a great new love for man and the world. The heart of the Bride and Mother which is aware of all the sufferings of individuals and societies on earth.

The People of God is a pilgrim along the ways of this world in an eschatological direction. It is making its pilgrimage towards the eternal Jerusalem, towards "the dwelling of God with men." God will there "wipe away every tear from their eyes, and death shall be no more, neither shall there be mourning nor crying nor pain any more, for the former things have passed away."

But at present "the former things" are still in existence. They it is that constitute the temporary setting of our pilgrimage.

For that reason we look towards "him who sits upon the throne and says, 'Behold, I make all things new.'" (*Rev.* 21:5).

And together with the Evangelist and Apostle we try to see with the eyes of faith "the new heaven and the new earth"; for the first heaven and the first earth have passed away.

But "the first heaven and the first earth" still exist about us and within us. We cannot ignore it. But this enables us to recognize what an immense grace was granted to us human beings when, in the midst of our pilgrimage, there shone forth on the horizon of the faith of our times this "great portent, a woman." (*Rev.* 12:1).

Yes, truly we can repeat: "O daughter, you are blessed by the Most High God above all women on earth . . . walking in the straight path before our God . . . you have avenged our ruin."

Truly, indeed, you are blessed.

Yes, here and throughout the Church, in the heart of every individual and in the world as a whole, may you be blessed, O Mary, our sweet Mother.

Dear Reader,

As if to underscore the Fatima Message, *on 13 May* God permitted an assassin's bullet to strike down His Vicar on earth, Pope John Paul II.

Why is it that the promise of Our Lady: "In the end my Immaculate Heart will triumph" has not yet been fulfilled? The answer is clear. God is waiting *until sufficient individuals* obey Our Lady of Fatima's call for personal conversion through prayer and penance. The divine revelation of Fatima stands at the heart of the mysterious conflict between good and evil in the world today, and the titles listed below are a brief selection from our current list, to help you gain a deeper understanding of this vital subject.

ALEXANDRINA by Francis Johnston
The remarkable life of a victim-soul for the Message of Fatima, who died in 1955. 27 illus.   120 pages

THE APPARITIONS OF FATIMA
A pocket summary of the principal apparitions and facts on Fatima, from Sr. Lucia's reports.   32 pages

FATIMA THE GREAT SIGN by Francis Johnston
The 5th printing of a recent best-seller which has been read by Pope John Paul II.   150 pages

FATIMA IN LUCIA'S OWN WORDS by Sr. Lucia
The last survivor of the three little seers graphically describes the apparitions. 21 illus.   206 pages

OUR LADY OF FATIMA'S PEACE PLAN FROM HEAVEN
An ideal pocket summary of the Message and its implementation. *Over 4 million copies printed since 1950.*
          32 pages

THE SECRET OF THE ROSARY by St. Louis de Montfort
An all-time classic, *over 1½ million copies sold since 1965.* Contains short, easy chapters.   120 pages

AUGUSTINE PUBLISHING CO., CHULMLEIGH, DEVON, EX18 7HL